EMOTIONAL
MANIPULATION

*All You Need to Know for Mastering Weapons
of Influence and the Art of Mind Control Using
Dark NLP, Brainwashing, Hypnosis, and
Persuasion Techniques*

By

Blake Reyes

TABLE OF CONTENTS

INTRODUCTION

As human beings, we respect one another. There are certain rules of life in society, rules of collaboration (you have to help each other to reach an objective), reciprocity (you have to know how to give as much as to receive), empathy (I put myself in the place of the other), trust and many others, which we apply daily.

You could say that the manipulator rather than respecting the collaboration rule, will try to get the other to do things for them. Rather than respecting the rules of reciprocity, they try to get the other to give to them, without giving in return. Rather than being attentive to what the other feels (empathy), they try to play the rule of empathy in one direction (if you do not give me what I want, you will make me suffer).

After all, the manipulator, and to put it a bit differently, does not consider the other as an end in itself, but considers them a means to gain personal benefit. They make a compliment, not just for the pleasure of the other, but because they hope to get something as well.

In extreme cases, for example, we find crooks or psychopaths (who sometimes are one), who play with intelligence on these social standards of reciprocity, trust, and collaboration.

We all manipulate others. But while respecting certain limits. It is a 'normal' aspect of human relationships. We will speak of a manipulator when the personality of an individual is globally organized around such social relationships. It is the constant character that makes the manipulator. Not the manipulation itself.

Some people, by their function, are likely to manipulate others. The word manipulation does not have the same meaning here! This is the case, for example, a manager leading a team and wishing to do it pleasantly and gently rather than by giving direct orders. Not always the healthiest mode of management, which seeks to conceal the relationship of authority, and which can be compared to an iron fist in a velvet glove. There are manipulative bosses, but because a boss asks you to do something without reciprocity, he does not manipulate you. Everything is, therefore, a matter of context. We will discuss all this in this eBook.

CHAPTER 1

WEAPONS OF INFLUENCE

Would you like to know how to influence other people? Who doesn't, right? Having the power to direct others' actions is something that many of us would like on some level. Knowing how to do it would be like a superpower, perhaps stronger than that of Superman. Just imagine being able to make your wife or husband do what you want. WOW.

Influence is probably one of the most frequently cited books in marketing for its accuracy in exploring the hidden forces behind the decisions we make.

Before exploring these weapons, we must take into account that the fundamental principle of this chapter is that, although many believe that we act rationally, this is far from the truth. Our decisions are mostly emotional. We are pre-programmed to act in certain ways, according to certain external stimuli.

Premise of Influence

By studying people with brain damage to their emotions, the famous neuroscientist Antonio Damasio showed that these people were practically normal, except that they couldn't make any decision. Despite being able to solve problems logically, when choosing, people are deprived of their emotions. These discoveries have caused a revolution in human behavior because they have allowed us to understand better how humans act. Under this premise, the first weapon of influence is reciprocity.

Reciprocity

An American scientist did the following experiment:

He sends Christmas cards by mail to strangers. To his surprise, most of the people he sends these cards to send him a card too. Why? We are pre-programmed to be reciprocal. If someone gives you a gift, you feel a sense of indebtedness and want to give something back. This is why we tend to reject gifts from companies that we know want to sell us something we don't want (maybe you rejected an air purifier from Rainbow vacuums?).

The force of reciprocity in action is very powerful, and it works, not only when we receive gifts, but when we feel some kind of indebtedness. For example, if I ask you to buy me tickets for a charity raffle for $ 5 and you tell me that you do not have $ 5 at that time. I could then ask you to buy me something of lesser value. How about a $ 1 bar of chocolate? The fact that you said "no" to me the first time can make you feel indebted and increase the probability that you will follow me if the second order is less.

Try it with your partner. Think of something you want and:

- Give him a gift
- Request something that you know he will say no to
- Wait a moment and ask for what you wanted

- The sense of reciprocity for the gift and the saying no will be so great that you have a good chance of receiving a yes.

Against this background, consider how you could use the weapon of reciprocity in your marketing and sales activities. For example, today, it is very common for companies to give free advice, an eBook, or downloadable help material, to start building a relationship in which the prospective client feels some kind of psychological indebtedness or a need to be reciprocal by buying something.

Commitment and Consistency

A Canadian study showed that immediately after gambling, people are more confident that they can win their bet than before. This seems simplistic, but it has profound implications. Humans have an almost obsessive instinct to be (or appear to be) consistent in our words and actions and maintain our status.

For example, once we state that we believe in a political idea publicly, it is extremely difficult for anyone to convince us to explore alternatives. On the contrary, in the face of any opposition, we will look for reasons to justify our belief. In the same way, when we identify with some group or ideology (people like us do things like these), we can become illogical in our decisions with the desire to be consistent and do things like we think our group does.

Do the following experiment. Ask your friends how many are considered collaborators. After their response (almost always yes), ask them to collaborate on something small.

Sure, your friends will be more likely to help after your question versus if you hadn't asked them anything previously. This is because consistency goes hand in hand with commitment.

When we take small steps (commitments) towards something, we gradually develop beliefs consistent with the steps we have taken. For example:

Q: Do you think drinking water is good for your health?

A: Yes.

Q: Do you think you are drinking enough water in a day?

A: No.

Q: Would you like to find ways to drink more water during the day?

A: Yes.

After only two questions (commitments), suddenly, the person being questioned wants to find ways to drink more water during the day. What would have happened if we asked the last question directly? The results would be mixed. The same is true for testimonials. Customers who give positive testimonials generally become fans of the products or services they testify about. After publicly saying something good about a product or company, they will defend their belief.

You should be careful in using this technique, as it is the tritest in the sales arsenal. It has been used a lot unethically by direct selling companies, and we are on the defensive when it comes to answering questions that lead us to commitments that we do not want to make. Anyway, used ethically and looking for the benefit of the consumer, this weapon of influence is super powerful.

Ask yourself, how can you make your prospective clients take small steps (actions or commitments) and gradual steps towards the purchase? What is the purchase journey that leads a prospective customer to become a customer? Also, consider what behaviors are most consistent with the personality or status of people like the clients you seek? For example, if your client is looking for luxury and your proposal is not consistent with luxury, no matter what kind of questions you ask, you will not be able to convince him/her.

Social Forces

You see someone laugh, and it makes you laugh. You see someone yawn and you yawn. In a stadium, everyone stops to make a wave, and you also stop. They are not just reflex effects. This is also a social influence.

When we feel uncertain about how to act, it is easiest to do it in a similar way to what other people do. This is why we buy items marked as "best-sellers," or we let ourselves be carried away by what the most popular figures say or do.

Nike Sponsorships offers are a great example. Nike has created a whole brand ideology behind the celebrity endorsement of each sport. Why are Jordan shoes so successful? Although we know, on a conscious level of Jordan shoes, they WILL NOT make us play like Michael, that MJ wears them is reason enough for us to want to buy them. True? It doesn't matter if other basketball shoes are identical at a fraction of the cost (a better logical decision).

To use social forces in your company, you can show your portfolio of satisfied customers, put certifications you have obtained and awards you have earned on your website, or even invite an influencer to use your products or services. The more you assure your prospective clients that other people in similar situations benefit from your offer, the more you can use this weapon of influence to your advantage.

Like or please

It is no surprise that we want to do business with people we like. It is also no surprise that we like things that we feel familiar with. What may be surprising is that "pleasing" or "being familiar" can be derived from repetition. For example, the more we listen to a new song, the more we like it. And once we like it, we buy it, we recommend it, and we even identify with its letter.

Why? Because it is a survival mechanism. Approaching the safe and familiar, as well as exploring the new and unknown, are part of us. Whenever something is unfamiliar, we have to experience it (see it, feel it, or hear it) several times to feel safe and to feel familiar.

Why do you say "YES" to someone who seems attractive to you? We tend to say yes to people we like physically more than people we don't like, because, generally, we like people who assimilate to a familiar face more than we consider beauty. We have a hidden need to want to please the people we like.

In this same sense, we tend to relate better with people with whom we share interests, antecedents, or points in common: SIMILARITIES. For example, we relate better to people who went to our same school even though they have not been our friends before, who like our same soccer team, or even who use the same brand of cell phone, simply because these similarities make us feel that we have things in common.

Here is the key to pleasing, what if you do not know what things you have in common with a prospective client? Simply frequenting places (where they can see your face several times), having continuous communication (such as emails where they see your name), and adopting mirror behaviors (reflecting movements and postures when meeting) are all "repetitions" that will make you more familiar to the moment to influence. Ask yourself: How can your company have more contact with the people or companies that you would like to reach?

Authority

Perhaps one of the easiest weapons of influence to understand is that of authority. In one experiment, social researchers asked an actor to make requests, similar to those made by a police officer, to passers-by on the street, requests such as picking up litter from the ground or not walking through certain sectors. The actor first made these requests dressed as normal and then dressed as a guard. The results?

When the actor was dressed as a guard, people obeyed his requests. But, when he was dressed normally, people saw no reason to fulfil his requests. This happens at all levels. For example, we trust the doctor's authority to the point that a white coat is sufficient for us to take medicines, of which we do not know their side effects.

We trust that a person dressed as a mechanic knows more about cars than we do, or that a person with a helmet and jeans on a construction site knows more about engineering than the average person. In a sense, we are programmed to trust authority.

But authority goes beyond what is apparent. For example, a study done in the San Francisco Bay found that car drivers whistle less for luxury cars when the light turns green than for cheap cars. Titles, clothing, vehicles, followers, are all signs of some kind of authority.

This is a topic of utmost importance for companies. If you are looking to grow your company, sell more with fewer objections, you must be an expert in your field. Ask yourself: how can you show authority?

Shortage

Last places. Only five items in stock. We have limited edition products. Make your pre-order today. These are all ways to demonstrate scarcity. The idea of a potential loss plays a fundamental role in our decisions, much greater than the idea of winning something.

Would you rather get a $5 discount or avoid being charged an extra $5 for a fine? In most cases, even though the result is the same, people would rather avoid losing than have a chance of winning. This is known as "loss aversion."

In an experiment by Stephen Worchel, volunteers were asked to give their opinion on a chocolate-chip cookie. The volunteers in one group were given one cookie, and they could see that there were ten more sample cookies. The other group was also given one cookie, but they saw that there were only two more sample cookies. The results? The group that saw fewer sample cookies rated the cookie better than the group that saw more sample cookies.

If your prospective client feels like they are going to lose something if they don't work with you, they will be much more likely not to let you go. Ask yourself how you can include scarcity elements in your offers. Prices or premium content, limited editions, exclusive programs, limited time offers, among others, are all actions that you can include in your commercial proposals.

When we make decisions, it is difficult to evaluate all our options logically. Generally, we use pieces of information that we consider relevant and make highly emotional calculations. Although each of the weapons of influence studied is valid, they usually do not happen in isolation. On the contrary, many elements are playing an important role simultaneously.

In this sense, to apply these concepts in business, we must visualize a global environment, taking into consideration the mission and vision of the company, and why a client would buy from our company and not from another. Once we have a clear picture of this, the application of weapons of influence can be ethically adapted within a process that helps generate a win-win situation.

The most Powerful Mind-Power Tool

You have the most effective resource for your journey to an enhanced life. Your mind is the tool.

Mindpower techniques can and will enrich your life.

Are you one of the many millions of people who are not satisfied with their lives?

Then there is hope.

Mind energy techniques are scientifically proven to improve the unconscious mind.

How can you be part of the most enriching phase of your life?

It is easy! Read on and see how you can increase the power of your subconscious mind.

Mental Power Techniques- Panorama

Just look around you at the wonders of modern society, technology, and development.

All those miracles are the creations of the human biological mind's most powerful tool.

You can imagine that the human mind has essentially no limits as to what it can achieve.

Supersonic airplanes, super aircraft carrier cargo ships, and automatic vehicle transmission engines all are the penultimate results of the power of thought and imagination.

A truly wonderful tool of the human mind has no limits to the progress and development it can generate.

A profoundly unfortunate fact is that the vast majority of individuals do not exploit the human mind's incredible capacity.

People of all ages and from all walks of life do not use the full potential of the mind, and there is a good chance that you are one of them.

How can you harness the full power of your mind?

Are there any power techniques that can be used?

Mental Power Techniques- Science And Medical Bases

The brain is a bioelectric machine. The impulses that are generated are the products of conscious and unconscious thought.

Your healthy and functioning mind generates electrical impulses, the healthiest thoughts in mind.

On the opposite side of the spectrum, those individuals who do not use or do not challenge their minds have a strong tendency to lose the benefits of it.

It would help if you exercised your mind to get the most out of the benefits it could give you.

Exercising- psychologically, which is the key to a healthy

mind.

However, it is very sad that most of the jobs and professions out there are just not conducive to exercising mind power.

Let's look at this example; the comparison of a gardener and an accountant.

The gardener uses less of his mental faculties in his line of work while the accountant solves countless complex math problems in daily work.

It's recommended that the gardener perform some recreational IQ or brainpower exercises to enhance brainpower.

His brain is enclosed in an imaginable hard protective skull layer.

The human skull can withstand a great deal of mechanical damage, but the brain cells it encapsulates can destroy a demanding and unhealthy lifestyle.

Life itself and the stress it generates creates detrimental factors for our brain capacity.

You may have previously experienced mental blockages, or you couldn't remember certain information when you needed it most.

Scientific studies have indicated that much of this is psychosomatic — it is caused by mental factors that are of your own free will and within your control.

This lower mental functioning is caused by low self-esteem and a negative global outlook on life.

So how can this be avoided?

Through exercise, and training through mental energy techniques, you preserve and improve your mental health.

Just as you exercise your body, so you must do mind training exercises to increase your conscious and subconscious mind.

Mind Energy Techniques To Promote A Better Life

Happiness and well-being are bi-products of the mind.

Your happiness and well-being are focused on your state of mental health.

A healthy mind is bodily sound — this is the wisdom of the ancient Greeks — which is still definitely true today.

There are proven methodologies today that have been shown to design or redesign your mental process.

Doing meditations and optimistic everyday affirmations are very powerful methods of mind energy to activate the subconscious' reprogramming cycle.

Meditation helps to calm down the brain activity of the conscious mind, which in turn opens the door to easily influence and impress more desirable thoughts in your subconscious mind.

Meditation also enables you to focus on a relaxed mind-state. A relaxed mood will give you the ability to stay focused, driven, and on track.

Furthermore, meditation is also highly recommended by the medical profession as a means of relieving tension and stress.

Strengthen the meditation process with daily positive and constructive affirmations that will give you a positive overview of yourself, your life, and your ability to achieve your goals.

Continuous repetition of affirmations to yourself during meditation will help you communicate to the power of your subconscious mind the positive thoughts and images of you living that life that you desire.

Audio technologies such as binaural beats have been seen emerging to change a person's mood.

They affect our brain waves directly through tones of different frequencies to aid our brain by improving brain function, motivation, memory, and more.

There are other techniques that you can use to harness the incredible powers of your mind, but just to get started, these are some simple but effective mind power techniques that can be used to propel your life to levels of unlimited success, happiness, and prosperity.

How To Increase Your Social Influence?

Social influence is the ability to awaken other people's behaviours, actions, and consumer desires. This social factor is the basis of Marketing strategies that use influential people to represent brands, helping these companies to gain engagement and generate more sales.

With the advancement of social networks as Marketing and business platforms, the importance of social influence has become increasingly clear to companies in their quest to understand and impact consumer behavior.

As long as brands know how to use this factor, it is possible to reach specific audiences and, above all, create genuine connections with their audience.

To influence others in favour of a business, it is necessary, first, to know well who you want to conquer, retain, or what the company's objective is.

From this, the strategy develops when there is a centralizing figure, someone capable of exercising this social influence on the public that your brand wants to impact.

Social influence has always played an important role in society and consumer relations, whether in simple opinion analysis or the chain reaction. Therefore, this section will cover the subject in detail and discuss the strategy and how it should be executed.

What is social influence?

Social influence is the ability to generate decisions and actions based on other people's behaviors, indications, habits, and customs.

Influencers, people who manage to rise to these movements, have a high power to generate repetition of their actions or to simply direct people to actions within a certain social niche.

This is a very common construction in society, and it has always been happening, no matter how few times it has been debated, until the emergence of digital influencers.

Each social niche has its influencer; that is why the ideas of influence are so broad and fit in so many scenarios.

Social influence as a strategy

A good example is the action of major suppliers in the sports sector, which sponsor not only football clubs, but also athletes.

Over the years, players have constantly appeared on the pitch with different cleats, always with different colours, shapes, and designs.

From a strategic point of view, brands have used this feature for years because they know the power of social influence that these athletes have, especially over fans of the team in which they play.

This rotation of boots is a way of associating a product with an influential figure, generating the desire to buy in people who are adept at the social niche in question.

The strategy is repeated in droves, in all possible markets and with actions from the simplest, as the example mentioned, to the most complex — more and more present in the digital age.

Without a doubt, it is the time for "digital influencers".

The rise of Influence Marketing thanks to digital

Marketing Influence is a strategy that has already been implemented for a few years now, the first place among the favourites of companies thanks to its effectiveness. The formula is simple: it is possible, with investment within the budget, to have an advantageous return, reaching the right audience.

There is simply no company that is unable to influence action, even though its audience is very small.

The micro-influencers are a category of people who can have a high level of social influence, even within a small niche. For many companies, this is enough to bring great results.

The high adherence to the strategy can be better understood in numbers. We separate some:

- In the USA, the ROI of campaigns with influencers is 6.5 (Tomoson);
- 49% of Americans claim to be influenced by a purchase (Influencer Orchestration Network);
- 8, out of 10 influencers, are micro-influencers; that is, they have 15 to 100 thousand followers.

How can social influence benefit companies?

Social influence, as the basis of Marketing strategies, can bring direct and essential benefits to companies that want to strengthen their brands and generate more sales.

More than gaining visibility, it is necessary to remain relevant in the market and count on the public's loyalty.

Understand how this strategy helps you achieve all these goals!

Accurate targeting

Social influence is the basis for strategies that put people as the "face" of their brands to generate the public's desire for consumption or, simply, sympathy.

The most important thing is not this power to influence, but who this influencer can reach.

The choice of this representative must be made in line with the target audience. It doesn't matter the size of the audience: the influencer has a great capacity to talk to whomever you want.

That is, an effective strategy provides highly accurate targeting. This ensures that the investment in the shares has an optimized ROI: the campaign will be able to generate more engagement and conversions, regardless of which ones.

Greater engagement

Followers are not always a faithful translation of your brand's growth. Often considered vanity metrics, these numbers do not necessarily represent what matters most: engagement.

This means that people are open to hearing about your brand, learning about new products, following everything that is launched, and consuming.

When social influence is high, the chances are high that this chosen figure will be able to transmit the message of your brand and, above all, generate a desire for consumption and replication of their attitudes.

While these people can be true curators within their

segments, they can also be brand ambassadors.

More sales

Sales are the most important and desired consequences. Although they are not the only ones since it is also important to ensure that the target audience is engaged and ready for more than an isolated purchase, companies depend on good sales.

The best way to generate your audience's desire for consumption is to use the capacity of social influence that someone has.

Whether using influencers or running campaigns in specific locations, especially those where your audience is and values, the chances of increasing sales increase.

Imagine that a certain brand has as its target audience the so-called geeks and decide to exhibit a new product in a Comic-Con Experience (CCXP).

The place, of course, is frequented by people from this niche and, being a specialized festival, creates a perfect environment for consumption. Through this strategy, the chances of generating social influence increase considerably.

What are the main ways to apply social influence in the Marketing strategy?

Social influence can be applied in Marketing strategies to generate results and make it possible to achieve the advantages that we have already discussed in this chapter. However, for this to be possible, it is essential to structure a plan and then start the work.

Next, through 4 tips, learn how to apply social influence in Marketing strategies using a complete and effective process!

1. Know your audience

Knowing the audience you want to influence is a priority requirement. This should be the starting point, and to further facilitate the understanding of who the brand's average consumer is, a persona well-defined is of great importance.

Only then is it possible to understand which traits of this audience can be exploited as triggers for consumption. Surveys are a great way to better understand the aspirations, preferences, expectations, requirements, and details of the average consumer.

A persona is built by analyzing a good volume of data in a relevant sample before the public. From this, it becomes easier to define a strategy to generate social influence.

2. Set goals

Companies have different objectives when implementing Marketing strategies.

Each brand can be at a different stage in the market, and that is precisely what will guide your intentions through campaigns and actions.

Thus, to decide how to exercise this social influence, it is first important to decide the objectives, the main ones being:

- increase brand engagement;
- increase e-commerce traffic;
- gain more followers on social networks;
- generate more sales;
- launch a new product.

3. Make the right choice of influencer

One of the most important parts of the strategy, the choice of the influencer needs to be someone who considers the factors that we have already covered throughout this chapter.

The impact of this person needs to be relevant within the niche, with adequate communication and the real ability to not only introduce brands or products but also to generate influence for consumption, concretely.

In this choice, it is also necessary to assess your audience's size, not just who these people are. The choice between large or micro-influencers is crucial since this segmentation is not always large and requires so much investment.

Remember: the chosen influencer must already have a previous relationship with the target audience, exercising the role of social influence.

4. Plan your actions

Once it has been decided who will be this brand ambassador, it is time to think about actions that promote the brand and its products.

Undoubtedly, posts on social networks such as Twitter,

Instagram, YouTube, and Facebook are the ones that give the most results today.

Different formats can perform well for each of them either in specific actions or in continuous campaigns, which have several presentations of brands and products.

Social influence is one of the great tools of persuasion that brands have to generate the desired impact on their target audience.

With the help of influencers, it is increasingly possible to create a legion of supporters of the brand and, of course, consumers.

CHAPTER 2

HOW TO INCREASE YOUR POWER WITH PSYCHOLOGICAL TRICKS

Some thoughts heal and others harm. The power of your mind can protect you like a fortress, and its absence, on the contrary, will make you fragile.

In addition to artificial intelligence, our natural intelligence can reach new heights. We are the first generation to benefit from the accelerations of time, space, and knowledge. We can move faster and faster and get all the information we want with one click. This speed leads to flexibility. The faster we evolve, the more we manage to carry out several operations simultaneously. But we must constantly adapt to stay in the race. You also need to know how to get out of your comfort zone. Education should give the child the desire to discover and venture into unknown territories. Sometimes, you have to embark on paths that seem closed and dangerous, but which can lead to other universes. These experiences will make you stronger, and you will, therefore, have an iron mind. You are the source of your invincible energy armor.

Your mom was blowing on your little sores to make them disappear, and it worked: you were no longer in pain. If you suffer from small daily ills today, do not rush to the drugs. You risk addiction, not to mention harmful side effects. Instead, learn to mentally "breathe" into these momentary pains. If you divert attention from what is hurting you, you will feel less harm. By focusing on one activity, you will forget the pain. For example, if you burned yourself lightly while cooking, try a new recipe that is a little difficult. After five minutes, you will no longer think about what should make you suffer.

It's proven, the body secretes its remedies to relieve itself. This is the case with endorphins, which are equivalents of morphine. Experiments have also shown that subjects relieved by a placebo (a fake medicine) have an increased level of endorphins, which makes it possible to erase the pain. Moreover, when developing a new drug, we know that just with the placebo effect, it will have at least 30% success.

Forgetting can make you smarter

Red squirrels have a habit of carefully hiding their supplies at the onset of winter, and then forgetting about them. Above all, do not panic if facts, names, places escape you. We immediately think of threatening specters like Alzheimer's disease or degenerative pathologies when this is often not the case. On the contrary, these oversights prove to be excellent for your brain. They allow memory to be erased to erase the least important details and focus on those that allow effective decision making. Forgetting is the tool for good memory storage, like computer hard disks, which have to eliminate data to store new ones.

Let's take an example: your doctor changes address. There is, therefore, no point in reminding you of the contact details of his former office. In other circumstances, you will erase memories of painful moments, which does a lot of good. When you happen to forget the name of a person, a film, a singer, ask yourself once found why you had temporarily erased it. Sometimes it's your subconscious that manifests itself to mean something to you. In his work, Psychopathology of Daily Life, which includes a chapter called "The forgetting of proper names," the famous Doctor Freud evokes his tendency to forget names or appointments. He interprets it as the unconscious expression of a repressed desire.

We get faster when the light is intense

Light can make us smarter, acting directly on our brains. We become faster when it is strong. American scientists have shown that under too weak lights, certain functions of our brain decrease in capacity. They discovered that staying in poorly lit rooms decreases our ability to learn and memorize. Thus, the researchers demonstrated that in a muskrat subjected to weak lightings, the hippocampus' capacity decreases by 30%. Located in the brain, the hippocampus plays a key role in memorization. The good news is that this impact is reversible. If rats having lived in the dark are exposed to powerful lighting, they recover their intellectual alertness after a certain time.

In children, scientists again noted that school performance was better in very well-lit classes. This is cured by exposing oneself to special lamps easily found in the market or by walking as much as possible outside as soon as the sun points at the tip of one's nose. Instead of looking for existential reasons when your morale is low, treat yourself with a light cure. A final example: after spending two hours in the darkroom of a cinema, some people find it difficult to remember where they parked their car. The memory is disturbed. We feel "funny" at the exit. According to the researchers, the lack of light slows down the production of orxin, the hormone that acts on the proper functioning of memory and learning. The impact of light on morale is well known. From November to March, some suffer from seasonal depressions due to lack of sun. This syndrome is called SAD. If you want to be successful and happy, put yourself in the light. You will shine intellectually and morally.

Learn to get stronger effortlessly

Is it possible to get stronger without exercise, simply by the power of the mind? Developing muscle mass without doing anything, sitting on your sofa watching television, looks like a science fiction dream. British scientists wanted to find out. They selected volunteers who did no more than two hours of exercise per week. They took measurements of the perimeter of the calves and their functionality, evaluated by electromyogram. The researchers then asked the participants to imagine that they contracted the calf muscles for fifteen minutes, 50 times in succession, after having indicated the force of contraction desired by small electric shocks. The volunteers had to repeat the exercise five times a week for a month. The results showed an 8% increase in muscle strength. This preliminary result opens up several areas for reflection. Imagining your muscles developing would unconsciously encourage you to mobilize them better later, for walking for example. Mentally anticipating what we are going to do improves the quality of the forces involved. Try to imagine yourself swimming: when you are at the pool or sea, you will evolve more efficiently. By adopting this method, you will become like these Olympic athletes mentally focused on the performance to be achieved, and then give the best of themselves.

Go in search of your dark side

There is something evil in you. Dare to recognize your dark side. You are sometimes selfish, manipulative, and mean. You are insensitive to the despair of others when they suffer or experience, on the contrary, a certain enjoyment in the face of the misfortune of others. You enjoy watching "disaster" news or movies in which poor victims are terrorized. You can even find a good side to bad boys. You laugh when someone stumbles and falls, not to mention questionable jokes, like reversing salt and pepper by watching the trapped one's disgust. You are, however, neither a psychopath nor a serial killer!

If you hide these trends in yourself, you might as well recognize them and not repress them. What we refuse to highlight always ends up being expressed: reactions of aggression and anger, flushes of anxiety which translate into self-destructive attitudes like obesity, tobacco or excess alcohol, missed acts... Instead of suffering, become an actor in your life by agreeing to explore these forbidden territories. It is not possible to help others by remaining comfortably on your couch, inactive. Devilish impulses can become a motor if one becomes aware of them. It is not a question of choosing a profession where you can abuse the limits of your power by making others suffer but from another dimension. Instead of looking at the victims as a happy spectator, recognize at this precise moment that your dark side is expressing itself. Then go beyond this reflex by thinking about the help you can bring. Your bad inclinations will serve as a spring to give birth to the best of yourself.

Your diabolical side is, in short, a potential of energy that only asks for a release to give meaning to your life and act on the world.

Alluring scams

It has become a global epidemic. The 2 billion smartphone users use a formidable function: image filters to erase imperfections and look more beautiful. Formerly reserved for professionals to correct the faults of stars, they are now in the public domain. What may seem like an innocent game is not. Boston scientists have discovered that these practices cause significant damage to the personality of users, affecting the overall image of their bodies.

These retouched photos, widely disseminated on social networks like Instagram, convey a false self-image. The more perfect they are, the more they move away from reality. This shift ends up creating dysmorphophobia, a syndrome consisting of being obsessed with imaginary faults and focusing only on one's small imperfections, magnifying them with a mental magnifying glass. This results in permanent stress and a decline in self-confidence, with the risk of social withdrawal. This phenomenon is particularly dangerous in adolescents, who are vulnerable and fragile in terms of the appearance they wish to give themselves. I advise not to pull the trigger of these fault correctors. Otherwise, when you meet people in "real life" after sending them these images, they will be disappointed. You will lose more confidence.

Instead, do the opposite. Find what you don't like in yourself, and make it a force to distinguish yourself. Think of Serge Gainsbourg's nose: if he had corrected it, he would have lost his exceptional personality. Value what you think are your faults, and you can climb mountains rather than hiding underground. If you love yourself as you are, others will love you too. You will live in reality, real feelings that bring joy and happiness. You will also sweep the artificial side that the company is trying to sell you. By removing the gap between what you appear and what you are, you will be doing yourself a favor.

CHAPTER 3

WHAT IS EMOTIONAL MANIPULATION?

For starters, there are many reasons why people feel the need to control people, places, and things, as well as to manipulate others to meet their personal needs, wants, and wishes. We must put to the surface the most common issues on the grounds of a battered ego with no self-esteem and, therefore, little autonomy. The people in control will always use manipulation tactics. It can be subtle techniques or master manipulators like many narcissistic personalities. Manipulation refers to the idea of trying to influence or control someone else's behavior or actions indirectly. As human beings, our pessimistic feelings sometimes affect our discernment so that it becomes impossible to see the truth behind hidden motives or intentions in different types of action. The controlling aspects of the complexity of perpetuating deception are linked to emotional manipulation, to lying techniques, and are sometimes very subtle and can easily be overlooked. Often, bad habits have been taken up through a negative ego that we have not worked on, whose control behaviors are driven away by feelings of guilt, low self-esteem, fears, and unethical behavior.

As the chaos generated by planetary ascent accelerates, many people are influenced by negative forces which they do not understand. Some of these negative forces come from their Unconscious and their Negative Ego, which have strengthened a life made up of negative habits and behaviors. When people feel insecure inside themselves, they will easily resort to controlling and manipulation behaviors. It is useful to educate yourself about this behavior to protect yourself and create the necessary healthy limits.

People who are in control will always assume that their needs, wants, and goals are more important than yours. No matter what you can do or your responsibilities, they claim that you need to focus on them and their problems, no matter what the cost may be.

Even if the cleverest of them aren't going to say it directly, the use of emotional manipulation will show you exactly what they're trying to accomplish. Through emotional manipulation, a person in control will use the empathy and compassion of others. He's a type of emotional vampire. Control behaviors are found in injured personalities of people who have low self-esteem, thoughts of fear. When these fears are not addressed and resolved, this need to control others can evolve into narcissistic behaviors and psychopaths.

The need to exercise control over others leads to the perpetuation of forms of manipulation. Manipulation of others leads to different degrees of deception and lying.

Motivation of Manipulators

What are the possible motivations of a manipulator?

- The need to put forward their own goals and personal gain no matter what it costs others;
- A strong need to reach feelings of acceptance,

power, and superiority about others;

- A desire and need to feel in control of people and the environment;
- A desire to gain a sense of power over others to increase their perception of self-esteem and worth in the world they create;
- A childish need to get what they want, coming from a high idea of themselves and no control over their impulses;
- The need to free themselves from inner anxiety and fear by projecting obligations on others to complete personal needs;
- The boredom of their environment, the desire to be entertained, or preoccupied with dramas.

Causes of manipulation

Why do some people so easily resort to emotional manipulation?

When a human being was never able to develop, from childhood to adulthood, with loving parents who support self-esteem and know how to set healthy boundaries, he will be easily manipulated. When someone is easily manipulated by their unhealed pain, violence, disability, and lack of self-love, he or she will become a cynical person with a damaged and fragile mental (suffering) body. Some individuals claim to be teenagers, but they are severely mentally damaged and go back to young, childish emotional states. Severe emotional wounds create a disconnection between the feelings of the soul and the spirit. Generally, the age at which the most unhealed trauma occurs in childhood is the age at which the adult returns when the injury is triggered in his adult life. When this accident is caused, most of the time, instead of taking responsibility for this suffering, the person assumes the need to exploit others because of their pain to get what they want. Then we can see a person acting like a little child having a crisis to get what they want. Both parents know what it's like to have a two-year-old kid who calls out, "To me! Give it to me!"

Most healthy people understand that pretending to act to feel a certain way, or to play with someone else's emotions, is not morally ethical. But some people are so preoccupied with what they want and have such a high idea of their importance that they are not aware of manipulating or deceiving others. Worse, some people have severe psychological schisms that create personality disorders that make them manipulate for fun. When dealing with narcissistic people and psychopaths, it is important to remember that they are masters in manipulation techniques and protect themselves against their antics. Set healthy boundaries and do not accept the emotional manipulations and dramas of other people, and make this a priority of your life, or they're going to assert what they're doing. It is important to be a loving and caring human being, but not a rug that is mistreated by psychic vampirism, which is the direct result of emotional and psychological manipulation. Many manipulation techniques are very intelligent, and we can be stunned by the layers of complex deception techniques. However, the more educated we are about this, the easier it is to be aware of this behavior in others and to get rid of it yourself. When we embark on the Krystic path, we must consciously stop using manipulation techniques and control behaviors over others. This will minimize the chance of using emotional manipulation repeatedly to vampirize the energies or control one's feelings of empathy for others. We also have the right to protect the room that belongs to us and to have the capacity to live without being used as a shield to exploit others. The obscure controllers are not in agreement with this freedom and are the promoters of this manipulation technique.

Common Handling Techniques

What are the most common manipulation techniques?

GUILT: Most of us know what it's like to be guilty of someone else; often, we learn this behavior from a family member early on. But many manipulators are gifted and cleverly making a person feel guilty when they are open at heart and compassionate. In general, this is like making you feel bad or sorry for something you have not done or for which you are not responsible. In the heart, in care, and giving to others, they must remember that their feelings and energies are also important. Often what you can give is not enough, so the manipulator will make you feel guilty to show you how bad you are because you didn't give him what he wanted, whenever he wanted. I have often noticed that when I do not jump when someone tells me to jump, he will use guilt with manipulation. It often happens in spiritual communities.

CLAIM TO WANT TO HELP: It is a big problem in all groups, communities, or organizations. It is undoubtedly a painful problem that we have faced in our community. Manipulators and bullies like to pretend to be useful even when it is not their real motivation. What they want is a feeling of control over something or having access to someone. There may be a desire for power, status, or personal goal that the person thinks they can achieve by claiming to be useful to someone else. Often these people create a lot of destruction and extra work on the pretext of being "useful." Then when the person/organization who is supposed to be receiving the help is left with additional problems, the person uses guilt to say how unappreciated and underestimated he is. Open communication and the assessment of qualifications and emotional maturity are a necessity in any organization that concerns a group.

NO RESPONSIBILITY: When we understand how manipulation works, we want to discern responsibility for the situation or the person. Manipulators will always blame others for their wrongdoing, bad behavior, or unhappiness. If they fall into narcissism, they may think they are perfect and beyond reproach. Putting an end to the manipulative blame game is the key to preventing this kind of deception from taking hold. If someone starts to blame you when they don't, don't be afraid of telling the truth.

DOUBLE SPEECH: Manipulators like to take anything that has been said and turn it around, or twist its meaning to use it against you. Often with manipulators who are good at the double talk, the conversation will be mixed with confused and ambiguous language that does not make sense. It is often a lot of words, without meaning or substance. Sometimes a part may make sense, but the rest of the conversation has no connection to what was said. Double talk is a lack of consistency; the person may appear intelligent by using certain words, but they are often either confused or trying to confuse others to prevent them from seeing the truth. You may have listened to this person to speak for an hour and have no idea what it is they're saying. It can also happen a lot in relationships with strong emotional ties, and it will destroy trust and intimacy between people.

PSYCHIC VAMPIRE: A psychic vampire is a person who drains the energies of others and can intentionally drain positive energy and happiness in the other. In the manipulation tactics used to make a generally happy person feel bad or take their energy, the vampire will use condescending and demeaning behaviors. They can use bullying and harassment to make the other person feel insecure or completely dependent on them. Generally, with these people, we feel that we have to take tweezers not to irritate this person, or to awaken their rage. You don't know what can trigger them at any moment. If you notice that energy is drained when a person enters the room, you should protect yourself and amplify your shield.

Setting healthy boundaries and being able to exist in the space where we can breathe, relax, and be comfortable with ourselves is the right we all have. Often as loving beings, we forget to take care of ourselves in the face of manipulative and controlling people. It is an important time to take care of yourself and to note that this phenomenon of control and manipulation will intensify in the environment due to fear, insecurity, and confusion among the masses. Many people have traumas and emotional crises and return to childish behaviors. Dark forces take advantage of this vulnerability in people who have not made an effort to understand and cleanse their negative ego. By becoming aware of how emotional manipulation works, make sure to end all of the manipulation behaviors within yourself. It's critical right now.

Types of Emotional Manipulation

We all want our needs to be met. However, manipulators use methods to fulfill their desires, and involuntarily, all the people around them, including those closest to them, become the means at their disposal to reach these desires. Often, this influence goes through a friendly tone. That's why it is worth learning to identify the main signs of manipulation so that you don't act as someone's puppet.

According to Jacques Regard, there are three types of manipulation distinguished by the specific and particular intention of the manipulator:

- Positive manipulation (known as "type I"), where the manipulator's intention is always good, useful, or pleasant for the person who is the subject of it.
- Egocentric manipulation (known as "type II"), where the manipulator turns the world around his

interests, without worrying about the consequences for his victims.

- Malicious manipulation (known as "type III") where the intention of the manipulator, of a paranoid, conscious and voluntary nature, is malice, the destruction of others.

Positive manipulation

This manipulation is not always perceived as a manipulation since its intention always appears good or pleasant. This is the case of a surprise made for a friend or a gift given to a child. This is also the case when a nurse says that everything will be fine before injection, that a mother uses gentle persuasion to encourage her son to do homework: "If you finish your homework this morning, you will have the whole afternoon to do whatever you want. Otherwise, you will have to spend the day there without being able to please yourself." Finally, this is also the case of an individual who seeks to show the positive aspects of something a priori unpleasant: "I'm going to have to come home late tonight, I have to stay at the office... It's annoying, but it will allow me to be on leave tomorrow noon, that way we can leave for the weekend earlier!" The manipulation is undeniable, but the intention always starts from the heart, it is not to be condemned, but it may be useful to recognize it.

Egocentric manipulation

In this type of manipulation, the manipulator is an individual who thinks only of his interests without caring either for others or for the discomfort that his conduct can generate. It is this manipulator who will do everything to sell encyclopedias to the elderly, without worrying about the interest of these, it is this manipulator who puts a stick in the wheels of his colleagues to make himself "seen well" to management or to get a promotion from them. It is this manipulator who makes promises with flying colors to be elected or this teacher, who terrifies his class to establish his authority. The type II manipulator does not act out of wickedness; he does not seek to harm anyone: but by thinking only of his interests, he inevitably harms others.

Marketing has become an expert in this type of manipulation for the customer to buy products.

When they were offered a sample of pizza at the entrance to their supermarket, one in two agreed to try it. But if the demonstrator touched their arm when making their tasting proposal, two out of three accepted their offer and especially twice as many then put the same brand of pizza in their shopping cart.

Malicious manipulation

This last type of manipulation is marked by the conscious and voluntary attempt by the manipulator to destroy others. Its purpose is to ruin the actions of an individual, to destroy an aspect of his personality, to harm his interests. It is a malicious and concealed intention.

Recognize a manipulator

Even if the manipulator can hide under very diverse and even familiar features, the author Jacques Regard has identified a certain number of characteristics and character traits that the manipulators can share.

- The manipulator is often imbued with excessive pride: he tends to belittle others.
- He regularly uses misinformation, lying, or slander.
- He insidiously harasses by never intervening directly, preferring to push others to act for him.
- He always pretends to act for a good cause and rarely recognizes his wrongs.
- He often speaks in a roundabout way, never asserting anything categorically but sowing doubt in others' minds.
- He spreads the rumors and conveys the worst slanders without ever giving the impression of doing so. He sometimes sends messages under the guise of frankness or clumsiness. He says nothing, repeats what he heard or what public rumor says.
- He is instantly angry when we try to unmask him. He does not assume his words or his deeds and turns everything to his advantage.
- He does not know how to listen to others' problems, except when it allows him to achieve one of his goals.
- He devalues a lot, often belittles with incredible balance, can contradict himself, or disavow what he just said a few minutes earlier.
- He likes to surround himself with incompetent people at work: "by rewarding those who work poorly, he ensures allies who are very devoted to him because, without him, they would be nothing."

- He depletes the energy of those who are in contact with him.

Manipulated?

Take this example:

For this year's Christmas, you have no intention of spending it with the family. Instead of your sister-in-law's devious reflections and your father's existential monologues, you prefer a romantic week in Marrakech. Personal desire versus family duty... Which of the two will prevail?

Julie, your best friend, asks you to lend her your car. Since you are going on vacation the day after tomorrow, you don't want to take any chances. You refuse. "Too bad," replies Julie. "I will not be able to go to this very important meeting for my job..." Worse still: "When you need help, I am always there." Immediately, you start to feel guilty ...

Attention, you are being manipulated! Besides, we all are. Just as we manipulate others in our turn, without necessarily being aware of it. Why? Quite simply to get the other to satisfy our desires. For this, guilt — or how to make the other responsible for our discomfort — is ideal.

Spot the blackmailers

The eternal victim

Let's take the family Christmas example again. Desiring to gather all her family on this occasion, the mother will sow doubt in her rebellious daughter: "You know, my darling, the family is sacred. We are getting old... Christmas together, there may not be many left... Your brother, he comes back from London, especially..." A classic case of emotional blackmail, with an implicit threat: "If you don't come, we will be very unhappy." The mother adopts the typical behavior of the "victim" to obtain the desired behavior from the other.

Susan Forward distinguishes four types of "blackmailers":

The executioner, who threatens to punish you ("If you leave me, you will no longer see the children").

The flagellant, who turns the threat against himself ("If you leave me, I commit suicide").

The martyr or the eternal victim, who brandishes his suffering ("How can you do this to your poor mother?").

The merchant of false hopes, who makes you dangle a promising future if you answer his request ("If you agree to set up this business with me, you will earn a lot of money").

The trapped gift

Another common process: the false gift. "By an abusive use of the principle of reciprocity — which is also essential for good social cohesion — the "donor" keeps the "recipient" in a debtor position. The implicit market is as follows: Since I gave you this, I have the right to demand that in return. The problem is that the donor chooses when and how the recipient must give him the change for his coin.

Example: a grandmother who, because she regularly takes care of her grandchildren, allows herself to land at her son's house unexpectedly as if she were at home. "How can I say no, she's so sweet!"

False Beliefs

Why is it so difficult for the person who is manipulated to react healthily? "Because the manipulator uses family and social beliefs to induce a heavy feeling of moral fault in his victim," says Isabelle Nazare-Aga.

Examples of typical beliefs: children are debtors of their parents (because the latter gave them life because they sacrificed themselves for them, etc.); it is in misfortune that one recognizes one's true friends...

"The guilt that the blackmailer instills in the minds of his victims undermines the positive image of themselves that they seek to build," explains Susan Forward. Abandonment, selfishness, injustice, betrayal are the sensitive points on which the manipulator presses to hurt. He often proceeds by innuendo. He never expresses a clear request and reduces you to impotence. Example: a sick mother, coughing very loudly on the phone, manages to slip in a sad tone to her daughter, that she has not eaten for three days because she does not dare to do her shopping. But, above all, she doesn't ask for anything...

Outsmart the traps

Get clear with yourself

Do a self-examination. Find the beliefs about yourself that spontaneously come to mind: I am selfish, ungrateful, I never measure up, I am worth nothing ...

Then stop focusing on the situation and try to change your perspective to make an objective statement about yourself: "Is it true that I am selfish?" "That's all I have done for her for three years... "; "Is it true that I am not up to the task?" "These are the elements that I can put to my credit..." Because the manipulator uses a single act of the person to judge him as a whole.

Then sort out what is and is not your responsibility: "Does his problem exist independently of me or am I really at its origin?" Indeed, the characteristic of the manipulator is to blur the boundaries by putting his needs before yours. "How far can I respond to his request while respecting myself?" Once you have assessed your limits, you will be able to make a clear decision. Two strategies are then available to you: counter-manipulation or confrontation.

Learn to counter manipulate

In order not to give a grip to the manipulator, do not justify yourself, because this would only weaken you even more. On the contrary, suggests Isabelle Nazare-Aga, simulate indifference — even if you are torn inside! — and refer him to his own beliefs with the help of a few calmly stated standard sentences:

"I have a clear conscience."

"Everyone does not think like you."

"That's your opinion."

"I do not think so."

"To each his own."

"Yes, I don't do anything like everyone else!"

The goal: protect yourself by not reacting to the provocations of your interlocutor.

Example: your friend Marianne, alone and depressed, accuses you of not having invited her during your last dinner.

"When you were bad, I introduced you to my friends; you let me down."

- It is not because I did not invite you to dinner that I let you down. When you need to talk to me on the phone or come to the house, I'm there.

- Yes, but that's the minimum a friend can do.

- If you don't value what I bring to you, it's a shame. I feel like you are demanding a refund from me for what you did for me.

- No, but, for you, it was not much to add cover. For me, it meant a lot.

- You count on your criteria what others must do for you. I'm sorry for you.

Dare to confront

This is the second possible strategy. Here, it is a question of referring the other to his need, therefore, to his responsibility. More implicating, the confrontation risks bringing you to position yourself on the nature of the link that you wish to maintain with the person who manipulates you.

Example: you are married, father of two young children and passionate about soccer, horse riding or tennis. Unfortunately, every time you plan to indulge your passion, your wife bullies you: "You leave me in the lurch with the children!" "Can you imagine if I did like you? ... "

"Any reproach expresses an indirect request," notes Jacques Salomé, author of To No Longer Live on The Planet Taire (Albin Michel, 1997). We must, therefore, try to get the other to formulate his need. "When you have fun without me, I feel abandoned, unloved." You can start a substantive discussion on the nature of your relationship: "Do I have to give up my passion to prove my love to you?"

"Doesn't the development of our relationship go through the well-being of each one?" This could also lead to negotiation on time spent together and separately, sharing of tasks, etc.

Refusing manipulation is accepting to pass for a "bad girl," a "selfish husband," a "difficult colleague." So give up an ideal self-image. You will do this by realizing your value. And it works. You may become less "lovable" in the manipulator's eyes, but by freeing yourself from this external gaze, you will gain a precious asset: your freedom.

Facing a tyrannical boss

Colleagues, little chefs, bosses... Everyone at the office manipulates everyone. Some calmly resist ("Sorry, but this week, I don't have time to deal with this additional file"), while others give in without saying a word for fear of being dismissed. How to achieve a modus vivendi with a boss who keeps imposing additional workloads on you? "Go for the temporary accommodation strategy," advises Susan Forward.

Here are the basic rules:

Do not tolerate anything that could harm your health — no question of accepting requests that would jeopardize your physical or mental balance.

Stay confident. Do a self-examination and see if you can improve the way you work or not to meet the new demand. The important thing is not to let negative beliefs undermine your views about yourself ("I'm too slow, I'm not up to par," etc.).

Consider modest actions that could improve the situation. Instead of rushing the confrontation with your boss, test the ground to clarify your position. For example, ask him to explain to you concretely what he would do to "get better organized" ... Or turn away from your usual behavior of submission by announcing to him that because of important projects planned for a long time, you will not be available when he needs you. Sometimes the worst tyrant finally gives in to face with determined resistance. And as paradoxical as it may seem, we thus force our respect.

What is gaslighting?

For Christel Petitcollin, communication and personal development trainer and author of numerous works on manipulation, gaslighting is extremely sneaky malice which aims to make the other pass for mad. The manipulator wrongly asserts things, denies facts. And then, sometimes, he compliments his victim, congratulates her. She then tells herself that she was wrong and that this person cannot want to hurt her. The manipulation also goes through the non-verbal. The aggressor can conceal or break objects to make it appear that the other is losing memory.

She remembers one of her patients who was harassed by her office manager. The latter had taken her glasses from her in her absence but claimed that it was not her and that it was ridiculous to accuse her. Difficult to go to complain to anyone. And then, why would she steal them? Her superior did not seem to have anything to envy her: she had a better job, a family life, a house... Something to make the employee doubt.

Victims gifted for happiness

According to Christel Petitcollin, these are high-end manipulators, completely aware of what they are doing. These people are "passive-aggressive," that is, they are full of anger, but they hide their hostility. They advance masked, using small vengeance, small aggressions. It is practiced in all environments with more or less finesse, explains the specialist. She describes these manipulators as immature people, like children in the playground, who enjoy mistreating others. And if they are exposed by their victim, far from stopping, they rejoice because they are untouchable.

Their favorite target? "Humanistic, open, kind people who do not see evil. They like to help others and flee conflicts. However, these manipulators hate optimistic people, gifted for happiness and joy because they are incapable of it", analyzes Christel Petitcollin. A profile that corresponded to the office worker harassed by her superior.

Gaslighting in a private setting with impunity

Gaslighting can also take place in the private sphere where the aggressor then has carte blanche, that is, a complete freedom to act as he wishes. Charlotte experienced this with her ex-boyfriend. "It was going well between us, Antoine was nice, and we loved each other. But soon after we moved in, I started to have doubts about myself, about my memory. I often lost things. As I am rather disorderly and head in the air, I thought that it came from me. I once waited for him in a cafe, but he never came. He told me that I had dreamed that we had an appointment. Sometimes Antoine told me that I had asked him to see such a film at the cinema when I didn't remember it. He said false things to our friends: that I was thinking of changing jobs, that I had seen such a girlfriend the other day... I was completely lost. By proof, I understood that he was the one who had a problem, and I left before going crazy," remembers the young woman.

Strong repercussions for victims

Depending on the situation, gaslighting can have significant repercussions. "Victims can develop post-traumatic stress symptoms that worsen over time. They can have sleep, eating, anxiety, tachycardia, or back pain disorders. It is destructive for the individual," warns Christel Petitcollin.

The solution to stop these manipulations, consists,

according to the expert, in cutting the links. "The aggressor becomes intoxicated with his abuses, which become a drug for him. He feels almighty. This can only get worse," added the specialist. The victim may feel alone in the face of the actions of this manipulator. This one advancing generally masked, the victim does not notice the problem.

Also, Christel Petitcollin laments the lack of psychologists' training in dealing with this subject, which is rarely discussed at university. Professionals can then think that the victim is paranoid and make a wrong diagnosis if they do not know these behaviors.

To keep all your reason and protect yourself against these potential manipulators, it is better to flee.

CHAPTER 4

SUBLIMINAL PERSUASION

Using subliminal techniques to persuade a person to do or buy something they may not need is a way to contaminate the subconscious psychologically. This type of pollution can become much more dangerous than you can find in the world's big industrial cities.

These "hidden" messages have managed to manipulate human behavior at surprisingly high levels, and worse, people have no awareness of being manipulated by such messages.

Subliminal propaganda experts manage to connect with our most intimate needs, impulses and emotions and play with our prejudices. All our activities and fantasies can be manipulated through our eyes and ears, from the most secret thoughts to the most public behaviors, without us knowing anything.

These subliminal messages and techniques, according to popular belief, Gonzales confirms, become increasingly dangerous, have been used over the years to idealize people's lives, making them believe that buying a Coca Cola is synonymous with buying happiness, or that with a Mercedes Benz the problems you have in your life will end. They take care of beautifying the basic needs of people in everyday life, from love, security and family, to work and pleasure, from such simple things to something perfected.

They show life in an "ideal" way. Everyone expects to be the exception to this rule and find that perfection is shown on television, in movies, series, and publicity on public roads when reality has little or nothing to do with those fantasies shown in different advertisements.

Both in film, on television and the different platforms used by the advertising, showing, for example, the perfect family: the slender, brave and cunning father who comes home to find his perfect wife, make-up on, smiling from ear to ear and waiting for him with the kids and the ready food table, big delicacies, all impeccable. Real families are far from like that.

Advertising strives to make the illusion more real than reality, and it is deliberately contributing to creating a world of unhappy and crazy people. In the ads, they propose as real, illusions that are only fantasies. The dangerous thing is that a lot of people start by believing it and end up blaming their clumsiness for not getting it. Information, which helps confuse reality with fantasy, is endangering a trait of psychic health: the ability to distinguish the real and the imagined.

When you buy a Dove soap or a Nivea face cream, you don't buy it because you're going to remove dirt and bacteria from the body or because it will nourish the skin well, but because in their advertising they show you the incomparable beauty and perfection that you can come to have used these products, then, what people buy is the ideal brand, not the product itself.

All these messages manipulate our choice when buying a product or service. It uses a subliminal psychological stimulation that has great effects on our decisions by managing to change them to the point of preferring that "hidden" meaning they show in advertisements.

This resource that attacks the subconscious affects not only a specific audience but also everyone equally, from the child to the young person, to the adult, and the older man.

Advertising specialists are well aware that the widespread sexual arousal that comes from a magazine with strong erotic content contributes powerfully to ads for cars, food, beverages, or perfumes and products of all kinds that include camouflaged sexual stimuli. The same is true of impulses, artificially activated, such as the desire to eat, drink, dress or acquire, when they are reinforced by the presence of stimuli associated with such motivations.

The most common ways of presenting subliminal messages can be seen through images that pass very quickly (tenths of a second) or with mixed or low-volume sounds immersed within a melody, so people do not realize that their subconscious is being maneuvered as it is virtually invisible to the eye or ear that send signals to the conscious mind, but not so for the unconscious, which captures every image and every sound.

The area of emotions, motivations, and needs of each person is the main objective in most cases, where it points primarily to all kinds of advertising to be able to reach.

Likewise, it is important to clarify that an isolated subliminal message has almost no influence on a person's life, but if the person is repetitively subjected to these messages, they do have a great effect (as in the case of people addicted to television, movies, or series). Similarly, if you receive positive subliminal messages, they will ultimately influence your daily work by literally transforming your life for the better, but this is not a very common case.

Subliminal advertising

Subliminal advertising began to be implemented since the early 1950s. This technique affects people, whether presented in a hearing, visual or written way and portrayed as necessary to improve the lives of these people as they often believe. These often lead to the constant search for happiness and perfection through the purchase of products, and they have nothing to do with these concepts, but they get to the point of convincing you that it certainly is.

The first known case of this type of publicity happened when James Vicary (1957) conducted an experiment where he included two frames per second in which he showed a mark that was in the event of advertising, in these frames were the messages "Come popcorn" and "Drink Coca-Cola" during the footage of a movie. These images that, though they appeared printed on the frames and were displayed on the screen, were not perceived by the viewer consciously, made sales of Coca-Cola and popcorn increase by 18% and 58%, respectively.

As Gonzales asserts, there are several studies and experiments conducted by universities over the years that have shown that advertising can modify the subconscious mind to ensure that it wants whatever it proposes in the transmitted messages.

On the one hand, on television are news programs that constantly remind of the evil and suffering in the world today, which happens daily in all parts of the world. On the other hand, there is commercial advertising that promises an ideal world, the perfect family, the perfect life, the perfect friends, in conclusion, a paradise of opulence that does not necessarily always show them as something material. In that world of perfections everywhere, every problem or frustration has its solution within reach of purchase, and a product or service can satiate anything you want.

The media recalls all the consumer's dissatisfactions, preferences, and yearnings, notifying him that there are unsurpassed professionals who have taken the job of coming to his aid and selling him the proper invention for little money. Advertising has everything, knows everything, and loves you. Advertisers are the envoys of the new religion in the antipodes of asceticism, duty, humanism, or any ideal that is the most sybarite hedonism. Advertising has dogmas such as progress, happiness, abundance, and leisure. It holds the secret of eternal youth, in an innocent world, without tragedies, without disease, and standards.

Numerous companies and brands use these psychological techniques to reach the target you want and influence your buying behavior without noticing. Some people consider this method unorthodox for causing stimuli in the person unconsciously and involuntarily.

Advertising is an incredibly lethal seduction, and it manages to realize all dreams and aspirations for a little money. However, this is not always virtuous, since it takes people away from reality by painting them a perfect world, a world that does not exist, an integrated utopia of pure brands.

Experts rely on studies where they analyze the yearnings and desires of individuals or societies to reach their unconscious and make them believe that they can offer them the perfect product to meet such needs, to the point of "training" recipients and instilling them with the acceptance and preference of certain brands.

Consumption is based mainly on the needs of each individual, which are considered as the engine of commercial activity, these can be innate needs, such as thirst, sleep, hunger, etc., or can be the needs learned or adapted throughout our lives, such as the value of money, the need for luxury, etc.

Subliminal advertising can become very subjective, that an image evokes something in someone does not mean that it also gets it in others; it depends a lot on the culture and teachings that each person has.

As unsold products accumulate, advertising needs to be more aggressive and use all of its resources. That's when subliminal advertising makes its appearance. An overly saturated market, if it wants to exit surpluses, ends up resorting to reinforcing traditional propaganda with subliminal techniques.

Being able to remember an ad is synonymous with the

effectiveness of it; however, this relationship of effectiveness in being able to remember an advertisement does not necessarily lead to the acquisition of the product, it must be borne in mind that the important thing is to motivate the change attitudes and to incentivize the purchase of it, which can lead to investing not only money but also time.

Conscious or supraliminal advertising tries to ensure your memory to assess its effectiveness. However, subliminal advertising is intended for the opposite: not to be identified or remembered on a conscious level. All the power of messages lies in the unmeasured; otherwise, they would turn against the one who uses them. The cause-and-effect relationship between advertising and sales is currently difficult to find out. It is even more difficult to separate the part that corresponds to the supraliminal and subliminal propaganda since they almost always go together. Of course, advertising has its part in sales. The advertising message is at the exclusive service of sales, which is its sole objective.

However, transparency and honesty are characteristic concepts of advertising. As much as advertising is not subliminal, it always has a deeper meaning beyond the one it shows. They always adorn and embellish the marks, which makes the information transmitted in advertising not truthful, as its main reason for existing is selling, not reporting.

Investment in advertising

Today brands, rather than being identified as a logo on a product or service, go far beyond that. Not only are they recognized for allowing you to recognize a product, but are generally associated with added values, which is achieved through the investment, adding values such as prestige, happiness, elegance, popularity or admiration.

A brand that is equal to quality with another brand can succeed against its competitor for two reasons; either it has lower prices, or has very good values added through advertising.

While advertising is responsible, among other things, for the above, it generally does not create an image of the products or services themselves, but the image of consumers of the products they advertise. This creates a perfect prototype for the consumer to feel identified, or want to feel identified. For example, the reason why men buy AXE deodorant is very likely not much because it is the deodorant with better quality and longer duration, but because it represents the figure of a man who in any situation is longed for by all women, which makes said deodorant, be parallel longed for by all men, wanting to be that boy chased by beautiful girls shown in brand advertisements.

The same goes for example, with the advertisements of the most prestigious perfumes, showing you a life of absolute ostentatiousness, elegance and prestige that only that perfume can offer you. Or the case of Red Bull is not the best energizer on the market, the most expensive, nor the cheapest, however, it is so well positioned by its advertisements with the slogan "Red Bull gives you wings" that when you think of energizers, it is the first one that comes to mind.

Often the choice of brand of a product is not due to its taste, its quality, or by some particular characteristic of the product, but in many cases depends neatly on external elements that are added by advertising. The preferences between products, in most cases, are clearly due to advertising and brand image.

The position of a detergent brand of the many advertised on television depends primarily on advertising. In this regard, what Durán (1982) states, an expert in psychology of advertising and sales: It is proven that there is a position for each brand of products in the same class. The individual, if he is interested in the advertised object, can retain seven marks in his mind. In order of its importance, the leading brand will be located on the upper rung. The fact of positioning is basic in any advertisement and is used as a communication strategy, although ideally, the brand of the advertised product reaches the position of leader.

Advertising has been advancing over time, adapting to the needs of the market. Both brands and consumers do not focus solely on qualities of the product advertised and its many benefits, but places attention on the target of the product and its potential consumers, creating an image of the consumer, representing him through a character with whom he can identify quickly.

A portion of the expenses invested in advertising is

intended to be fair, market research, and types of techniques that may become more effective in significantly influencing consumer behavior, making them want the product that's advertised.

This can lead a person to choose a brand from many existing products in the same type, and with the same characteristics. It is emotional engagement and positioning that creates that mark with the target. It's all about buying the people's emotions; emotions can be much more powerful and effective to make the consumer decide on your product instead of choosing the one from the competition. The creation of that brand-client link is made possible by advertising.

Brands need to know that when they decide to invest in advertising, not only are they paying for a spot on television, an ad in a magazine, a newspaper, a track on the radio, or the internet. Rather, they are investing in the establishment of this link, which once it is well-positioned in the consumer's mind, is very difficult to break overnight.

The financing of subliminal advertising is one of several methods that exist to lead to the success of a brand, everything is based on its effectiveness and the techniques used to reach the subconscious of the individual, which is not always very simple to achieve, so both large industries and advertising agencies, for the most part, have their research laboratories of these phenomena.

One of the inexcusable factors for the subliminal techniques chosen to fulfill their purpose well is that their true objectives are not revealed by "showing" themselves in a message.

In a brand-rich society, where new competitors are always emerging with products equal to each other, with better price, better presentation, or simply almost undifferentiated to each other, it is very important to know how to make a path to triumph in the market. For that, you have to know very well how the product is better and what to allocate money to that will place the campaign of a product that aims to be victorious in the Market.

The Basics of Persuasion

In general, persuasion can be understood as a form of strategic communication that aims to convince other people. Through persuasion, it is possible to induce someone to assume a certain position, perform a specific task, or accept an idea.

This communication includes an adequate posture, emotional appeals, and, mainly, a strong and logical argument. In this way, it is easy to see that the psychology of persuasion is associated with some basic topics such as knowledge, rhetoric, and image.

This competence is important for everyone, regardless of profession or industry, but it becomes even more essential for leadership positions, sales professionals, and those who work on projects. And, like most behavioral skills, it can be assimilated and improved.

Methods of Persuasion

The individual can develop this communication capacity to persuade the actions and decisions of others.

Based on his studies, Robert Cialdini created the persuasive communication theory, which is based on the concept of taking advantage of some patterns of conduct internalized collectively, to suggest behaviors. This theory lists the six principles of the psychology of persuasion, which can be taught, learned, and applied. They are:

Reciprocity

This principle defines that people are more willing to agree to a request when they have already received something in return. Social norms encourage us to respond positively to those who have done us a favor or helped us at some other time.

Consistency

The individual is also more likely to follow a pattern if he thinks that this model is consistent with his ideals and values.

Authority

According to this principle, the authority and seniority transmitted by the communicator determine factors for others to feel predisposed to approve or validate something. At this point, the communicator's argument and stance have a special emphasis.

Social Validation

According to Cialdini, the greater the common sense

regarding a behavior, the greater the likelihood that someone will adopt attitudes that fit this pattern.

Scarcity

In this principle, the author reiterates that the charm generated by a product, service, or situation is inversely proportional to its availability. That is, the scarcer, the more relevant.

Friendship/friendliness

Finally, the sixth principle indicates that people are more inclined to collaborate or agree with others when there is an identification, a friendship relationship, or some attraction.

It is worth remembering that the principles of Robert Cialdini's influence should not be used autonomously, but combined, as part of more efficient and provocative communication.

The strength of the argument

The argument, in turn, is based on coherence and uses real facts to consolidate a thesis. A good argument is full of examples, data, technical studies, research, and comparisons, to prove the truth of a statement or the viability of a proposal.

Thus, the communicator can involve others, making everyone start following the same line of reasoning until they are persuaded.

This power of persuasion is significantly increased when the argument is joined with empathy. In this case, it is possible to create a communication that mixes reason and emotion, reaching the main centers of convincing.

Persuasion in the corporate universe

It is easy to see that relationships have become increasingly virtual and, often, less productive. This movement is caused not only by the advancement of technology but also by the underutilization of important skills.

Among these skills are empathy and the ability to argue, which together can ensure healthier and more collaborative relationships, especially in the corporate environment — where peaceful coexistence between professionals with the most diverse profiles is a basic need.

Individualism has become a major problem, hampering teamwork and collectivity. Therefore, care must be taken with the virtualization of communication and the almost exclusive use of e-mails, messaging applications, and social networks.

It is also important to consider that dialogue is an efficient way to perceive fears, motivations, and needs, normally hidden in fully digital communication. Personal contact creates ideal conditions for feedback, negotiation, guidance, advice, and convincing.

Also, the correct application of the psychology of persuasion is one of the main characteristics of true leaders, who manage to inspire and engage their teams. Therefore, this issue must be present in the leadership preparation program. With a powerful argument, it is possible to induce critical thinking — a fundamental ingredient for the formation of high-performance teams. The results will be even better if the communicator is recognized for the positive reference that inspires others.

CHAPTER 5

WHAT IS NLP? (NEURO-LINGUISTIC PROGRAMMING)

"A model of choice and therefore of freedom," "A philosophy of life," "A way of organizing and sequencing our thinking."

What is NLP?

NLP (Neuro-Linguistic Programming) is an approach in psychology. It is a pragmatic approach to communication and change. It focuses on "how to make it work." NLP can be articulated in three different aspects:

1. The essence of NLP is modeling what humans can do best. The process is to "learn from others."

2. The use of modeling gives rise to a large number of techniques.

3. NLP has also developed a certain way of looking at the world and life. It's a bit of a philosophy that advocates human development, autonomy, freedom of thought, ability to relate to others, openness to difference, tolerance.

NLP is a new approach to human functioning, the fruit of the mixing of ideas, and the confrontation of passionate researchers from various disciplines.

It offers an original synthesis leading to immediate use of the knowledge of psychology and neuroscience, anthropology, and artificial intelligence and management.

We are interested in "how it works when it works" rather than explaining "why it doesn't work." It makes it possible to decode the experience of people who are particularly gifted in a specific field (negotiation, communication, education, sport, health, therapy...) or who, placed in difficult situations, have discovered unusual and effective means of getting out of it (transform phobic or traumatic responses, get rid of unwanted behaviors like insomnia, bulimia, and parasitic emotions like jealousy, anxiety, lack of self-confidence).

When we have decoded all the how's of a behavior or a strategy of excellence, identified the components of someone's "talent," whether it is a way of being or a skill, NLP allows us to acquire this capacity for ourselves or to teach it to others.

Who is NLP for?

For all helping relationship professionals who want their clients to make faster, easier, and more predictable progress. For all professional communicators: managers, heads of personnel, executives, salespeople, etc. For all teachers and parents who want to give themselves the tools necessary for quality educational communication. For all humans concerned with the development and harmonization of their internal and external resources.

Discover the basics of NLP!

What can NLP do for you?

Modelization

Decode what specifically other people do to perform in a field: sport, business, education, therapy.

Education

Learn to use the skills decoded among experts, artists, or artisans in a field that interests you — having access to your resources when it matters most: before a meeting or an important presentation when an unforeseen event destabilizes you. Develop a real quality of relationship with your friends and colleagues.

Communication

Develop your communication skills and get better results, professionally and personally. Resolve conflicts between people, your internal contradictions, or those of others.

Transformation

Develop your value systems, belief systems, self-concept during life transitions, major changes in your environment (emotional, socio-professional, etc.). Help others to modify their behaviors, thinking strategies, beliefs, and the resulting emotions to facilitate their personal and professional development. Help companies, organizations, and social systems develop concrete tools to manage change and future challenges.

NLP Training

You might wonder what's going on in NLP school if you're one of those who aren't so familiar with NLP. If you are enrolled in NLP training, you will be in a program that can enhance the connection of extensive neurological processes, self-confidence, linguistics, and skills between the existing links. Some training programs say they will help you develop a new sense of self-awareness and self-esteem that will lead you, particularly in your profession, to new heights for your life. However, one point that has to be known is that NLP preparation is not meant to identify or cure psychological conditions; it merely reflects on the issues that the individual has and how to solve those "issues" to progress.

Most experts will say that realistic and hands-on teaching is the perfect form of studying Neuro-Linguistic Programming, much like any other study. Trainers or coaches most often use a unique training style, which includes humor and playfulness. The problem now is: What is NLP Teaching doing? One NLP Training Provider claims their programs provide their students with the skills, techniques, and knowledge to effectively create positive results that can transform their lives for the better. Just think if you're enrolling in one of these NLP Training programs, you're going to get a chance to become someone who's having amazing opportunities. You'll now have the chance to change your negative actions and turn it into something positive. Also, some NLP Training Programs teach you leadership skills and management preparation to take full responsibility for your life and learn to guide others to the improvements you want.

Even though there are many good and positive things one can get from joining an NLP Training, there are still some program critics. That, by the way, is natural and cannot be avoided; that is valid for any productive program. One major critic is that NLP therapists are only in fraud or that the NLP itself is a scam. I don't think NLP is a scam, but certain clinicians are highly doubtful and should be handled carefully. Also, there are so many untrained practitioners out there, so to prevent these things from happening, one needs to conduct research.

By joining NLP training courses, you'll be able to see the path you're on. You will be put in the right direction by fresh and creative thinking, and NLP Learning always helps you understand the broader horizons of life. Also, NLP is an effective way to assist you in interpersonal relations, including your job and education. It also lets you improve the way you teach business deals, among many more in your everyday life.

CHAPTER 6

BRAINWASHING & HYPNOTIC PROCESS

In 1962 the first version of The Messenger of Fear was released, a film directed by John Frankenheimer that had actors such as Frank Sinatra, Laurence Harvey, or Angela Landsbury. Released in the middle of the Cold War, at the same time as the missile crisis was taking place, the film tells how a Korean War soldier returns home to receive the highest award from the US Congress for his heroism. Little by little, he realizes that both he and his companions suffer nightmares and have strange behaviors. As a result of those nightmares, an investigation begins where little by little, it is discovered that the protagonist has been subjected to brainwashing, being the victim of an international conspiracy to commit a criminal act that may influence the politics of the United States. We are not going to reveal much more about the plot. In reality, it is too tangled, devoid of all logic and not without a certain conspiratorial paranoia, at least in its final twenty minutes. The film is valuable for its performances, for reflecting a theme that had its boom during the Cold War years, and for maintaining a plot very well carried out by actors and screenwriters until almost the end. [In 2004, Jonathan Demme made a worthy remake of this movie.]

Can you brainwash a person to commit all kinds of acts,

including murder?

Can hypnosis program a person's brain to commit any act unintentionally?

In the early 1950s, millions of Americans began to ask themselves these questions when they were able to see Hungarian Cardinal József Mindszenty, with a face that seemed hypnotized, confidently confess all the crimes he was accused of by the Stalinist government. The next thing was to see hundreds of American soldiers who had been captured by the North Korean army sign declarations in which they blamed themselves for all kinds of crimes, and requested the withdrawal of American troops from the war and denouncing the use of bacteriological weapons. Public opinion in the United States was not surprising, especially when many of these soldiers continued to hold the same opinions after returning home. What have they done to our boys? Many wondered.

In 1950, a CIA-linked journalist, Edward Hunter, began publishing a whole series of articles and books on the techniques used in Stalinist regimes to get a person's brainwashing. This expression began to be used for the first time then.

In 1951 the ARTICHOKE project was created that would become, under the command of Allen Dulles, director of the CIA, Operation MK Ultra, to obtain methods that would achieve control of the human mind. From the beginning, numerous investigations in different universities and research centers were financed to achieve, almost always through hypnosis, electric shocks, and the use of drugs such as LSD, purposes related to espionage in the Cold War. They had three objectives: to obtain all kinds of information from the captured spies, to create spies incapable of revealing secrets and, finally, to create programmed soldiers, capable of executing a murder at a certain moment and without knowing it consciously. The latter would be the 'Manchurian candidates'. Many millions of dollars were spent on this project to win the Cold War in the field of espionage. However, by the mid-1960s, many investigations had already been canceled due to the poor — and often counterproductive — results obtained.

At first, so much hope was put into hypnosis that even ARTICHOKE member Morse Allen himself attended a course taught by a famed New York hypnotist. Impressed by the enormous possibilities of hypnosis, he began practicing with his secretaries. The results were more than acceptable, by making one try to assassinate his partner following his orders. However, it was one thing to hypnotize a secretary, conditioned by his boss and the trust he placed in the institution where he worked, and quite another to hypnotize someone, program them to commit a crime, and get them to carry it out finally.

Not all subjects were good candidates for these techniques, and it was never clear if they would eventually be able to commit the act for which they were scheduled, bearing in mind that when executing it, they could be thousands of kilometers away from their hypnotized person. Who would be the person giving the order then? What if he acted by chance to hear the key phrase at the wrong time? It was one thing to hypnotize an individual so that they would then commit an act and quite another to be able to program it, leaving their faculties intact, to commit a crime at a precise moment. As John Gittinger, director of the MK Ultra, noted: "You cannot predict absolute control of a subject; any psychologist, or any psychiatrist, or any preacher, has relative control over certain individuals, but can never predict their reactions; there is the question. It looks like it was tried, but John Marks, author of In Search of the Manchurian candidate, where he documents all these investigations carried out by the CIA, does not confirm that nothing definitive of these projects was achieved. It even seemed like there were simpler methods for an assassin to kill someone without subsequently revealing any information if caught. The 638 attempts to assassinate Fidel Castro by the CIA demonstrate this. They tried everything, even if they were not successful.

The truth is that many of these investigations were carried out with unorthodox methods, even for the time. Doctors like Ewen Cameron did not hesitate to apply sensory deprivation to their patients for weeks, which, together with the stimulation with electroshocks and the administration of sedative drugs, ended up causing irreversible episodes of amnesia without, on the other hand, the disease to be treated (schizophrenia). These attempts at behavior modification through the deconstruction of the personality were very aggressive and with few results, but the CIA was very interested in its financing. The 'truth serum' and the application of the same

Stalinist techniques to a Russian in the Nosenko case also failed. This ex-spy, who spent 1277 days under isolation and interrogation, did not reveal any conclusive evidence. As the CIA was not clear whether Nosenko was telling the truth, the Stalinist techniques did not work.

But then how did the Soviets get Cardinal Mindszenty to confess to any crime or get American soldiers caught in Korea to sign those statements? Harold Wolff, a neurologist and personal friend of Allen Dulles and his collaborator at Cornell University, Lawrence Hinkle, led a research group that collected all kinds of information, especially from former KGB members who knew the techniques perfectly well. That the detainees and the tortured themselves were subjected. In 1957, Wolff and Hinkle showed in their work that the Soviet techniques were based on a constant and overwhelming physical and psychological pressure, without further ado, which mainly affected the weakest aspects of the human structure.

In short, the method was as follows: the prisoner was subjected to rigorous isolation in his cell, without being able to communicate with anyone or anything. During this isolation, he was often forced to stand up, woke up in the middle of the night, and the guards beat him for no reason. After a few weeks, the interrogations began while a prisoner, totally exhausted, saw his interrogator as the only person who had spoken to him in a long time and, wishing to end everything, ended up signing anything. According to former KGB members, the detainee was considered guilty; it was only a matter of time that he ended up signing his confession, which was achieved in a few weeks in most cases. The method was not trying to reveal the truth.

The Cold War encouraged many writers to write works that seemed almost science fiction. The idea of a programmed killer has been recurring in the cinema for decades. In 1965 Michael Caine was brainwashed by waves in Sidney J. Furie's Confidential Archive. In 1977, on Phone, an always tough Charles Bronson would have to discover the person activating the programmed assassins, that the Soviet Union had scattered throughout the United States. Pure paranoia of the Cold War? Undoubtedly, but the idea of a candidate from Manchuria gave a lot of play so that the film industry did not take advantage of it. However, the human mind is still much more complex, and its control seems less easy than many would like.

China and the Korean War

Initially, the Chinese term "brainwash" was used to describe the coercive persuasion used in China under the Maoist government to transform "reactionary" people into "well-thinking" members of China's new social system. The term made puns in the Taoist custom of "cleansing/washing of the heart/mind" (xǐxīn, 洗 心) before performing ceremonies or entering holy places.

The Oxford Dictionary of English documents the oldest recorded English use of the term "brainwashing" in an article published on September 24, 1950, by journalist Edward Hunter, in Miami News. Hunter was an ardent anti-communist and is believed to be an undercover CIA agent posing as a journalist. The Hunter and others used the Chinese term to describe some American prisoners of war (POWs) who cooperated during the Korean War with their Chinese captors (1950-1953), even crossing over to their side in some instances. British radio operator Robert W. Ford and British Army colonel James Carne also said the Chinese had brainwashed them during their imprisonment in wartime.

The United States Army and government put brainwashing charges to undermine confessions made by prisoners of war to war crimes, including biological warfare. After Chinese radio broadcasts asked Frank Schwable, Chief of Staff of the Air Wing First Navy, to participate in bacteriological warfare, United Nations Commander for General Mark W. Clark stated:

It is doubtful whether these statements passed those unfortunate lips each time they passed. However, if they did, all too familiar is the mind that annihilates these communist methods of extorting whatever word they want... The men are not to blame themselves and have my sincere remorse for being used in this abominable way.

Starting in 1953, Robert Jay Lifton interviewed American soldiers who had been war captives during the Korean War, as well as priests, professors, and teachers who had been held in China after 1951. Lifton interviewed 15 Chinese people who had left Chinese universities after being exposed to indoctrination, in addition to interviews with 25 Americans and European people. (Lifton 's 1961 book Reform of Thought and Totalism Psychology: An Analysis of

"Brainwashing" in China, based on this research.) Lifton found that when the prisoners returned to the United States, their behavior gradually returned to normal, unlike the common image of "brainwashing."

In 1956, after re-examining the concept of brainwashing after the Korean War, the United States Army released a report titled Communist Interrogation, Indoctrination, and Exploitation of Prisoners of War, which demanded to brainwash. Brain "popular belief." The report states that "a thorough investigation by various government agencies did not reveal a conclusively documented case of 'brainwashing' of a US prisoner of war in Korea."

In George Orwell's 1949 dystopian novel Nine Hundred and Eighty-Four, the main character is subjected to prison, isolation, and torture to confirm his thoughts and emotions to the wishes of the future rulers of Orwell's fictional totalitarian society. The vision of Orwell inspired Hunter, and is now mirrored in the mainstream perception of the brainwashing idea. Written around the same time, JRR Tolkien's The Lord of the Rings also addressed brainwashing, albeit in a fantasy setting. Cordwainer Smith's science fiction stories (written from the 1940s until he died in 1966) depict brainwashing as a natural and benevolent aspect of potential medical procedure to erase the memory of stressful events.

In the 1950s, many American movies were filmed, which included brainwashing of POWs, including the shelf, prison bamboo, Into the Unknown, and the Fearmakers. Forbidden told the story of Soviet secret agents who had been brainwashed through classical conditioning by their own government so that their identity would not be revealed. In 1962, The Messenger of Fear (1959 based on the Richard Condon novel) "put brainwashing ahead and center" by presenting a plot by the Soviet government to take over the United States by using a brainwashing presidential candidate. Brainwashing was popularly associated with research by Russian psychologist Ivan Pavlov, who mostly involved dogs, not humans, as subjects. In The Messenger of Fear, the head Brainwasher is Dr. Yen Lo of the Pavlov Institute.

In science fiction, mental regulation is still a big subject. Terry O'Brien said: "Mind control is such a strong concept that no hypnosis, then something similar ought to have been invented: the plot is too useful for any writer to ignore the fear of mind control, just as powerful an image." A subgenre is corporate mind control, where companies that rule society through advertisements are controlling a future society.

American government investigation

For twenty years since the 1950s, the United States Central Intelligence Agency (CIA) and the United States Department of Defense conducted a secret investigation, including Project MKUltra, to develop practical techniques for brainwash; outcomes are unknown. CIA studies using various psychedelic substances, such as LSD and mescaline, were based on Nazi human experimentation.

In 1974, a member of the affluent Hearst family, Patty

Hearst, was abducted by a left-wing organization named the Symbionan Liberation Army. After several weeks in captivity, he agreed to join the group and participated in their activities. In 1975, he was arrested and charged with bank robbery and the use of a firearm in the commission of a serious crime. His attorney, F. Lee Bailey, argued at trial that he should not be held responsible for his actions since his captors' treatment was equivalent to the Korean War prisoners of war brainwashing. Hearst was found guilty, but his "brainwashing defense" brought the issue to the attention of the renewed public in the United States, like Charles Manson 's case of 1969-1971, who was alleged to have brainwashed his followers for murder and other crimes.

Bailey developed her case in conjunction with psychiatrist Louis Jolyon West and psychologist Margaret Singer. The two had studied the experiences of the Korean War prisoners of war. In 1996 Cantor published his theories in his biggest sale of books, Cults in Our Environment. In 2003, the brainwashing tactic was misused in favor of Lee Boyd Malvo, convicted of murder for his role in the DC sniper attacks. Several legal scholars argued that brainwashing security violates the fundamental principle of free will regulation.

Italy had a dispute about the definition of plagiarism, a crime consisting of an absolute physical-psychological environment, and eventually an individual. It is said that the consequence is the destruction of the problem of equality and self-determination and the consequent rejection of his identity. The plagiarism offense has been seldom charged in Italy, and only one person has ever been arrested. In 1981, an Italian court found the concept to be imprecise, lack coherence, and subject to arbitrary use. By the 21st century of child care and child sexual assault, the idea of brainwashing is being implemented "with considerable effectiveness." In some cases, "one parent is charged with brainwashing the child for refusing the other parent, and in child abuse cases where one parent is charged with brainwashing the child for making charges of sexual abuse against the other parent" (possibly resulting from or causing alienation of the parent).

In 2003, forensic psychologist Dick Anthony said, "No reasonable person doubts that there are situations in which people can be influenced against their interests, but those arguments are evaluated based on fact, not false testimony from an expert." In 2016, the Israeli anthropologist for religion and his companion at the Jerusalem Van Leer Institute Adam Klin-Oron said of the then proposed "anti-cult" legislation:

There was a surge of 'brainwashing' allegations in the 1980s. Then parliaments around the world looked into the issue, and courts around the world looked into the issue and came to a strong conclusion: No, there is such a thing as cults ... that the people who make these claims are often not adept at it. And in the final courts, including in Israel, rejected experts who affirmed that there is "brainwashing".

Lifton's eight criteria for thought reform

Milieu Management is a concept popularized by psychiatrist Robert Jay Lifton to describe strategies that regulate the environment and human speech by using social coercion and group language; these strategies can include ideology, advice, vocabulary, and pronunciation, allowing group members to recognize other members or facilitate cognitive improvements in individuals. Originally, Lifton used "milieu control" to describe brainwashing and mind control, but the term was already used in other contexts.

In his book, Dr. Lifton identified eight main themes or criteria for detecting, evaluating "ideological totalitarianism" and its implementation in groups, institutions, and others. These are not manipulation recipes but symptoms to judge its existence. Of course, things are never so clear in reality. It should also be borne in mind that this is not a theory but an attempt at classification made based on dozens of hours of interview with people just released from the totalitarian environment where they had been "reformed."

The more an environment presents these eight psychological themes, the more it resembles ideological totalitarianism ...

1. Control of the environment

... It is obvious, but this control is more or less visible: from physical confinement — prison — through "Revolutionary University" to, sometimes, an entire country. This control is essentially that of communication, not only of each individual with the outside but also with himself. George Orwell, as a good Westerner, imagined the control using a device — a permanent, two-way television, each being recorded at the same time as it received the broadcasts. The Chinese, on the other hand, used human instruments.

As perfect as this control — material or psychological, or both — may be, it is never absolute. There can always be, from the outside world or from the subject itself, "parasitic" information interfering with the messages of the manipulators. For those who apply the system, if they cannot create an environment containing only their truth be told, they attribute these inadequacies to an imperfect application of the procedures and the total perversity of the refractory. For the latter, the ultimate consequence is his physical elimination; but this itself constitutes a personal failure for the manipulators. They have themselves been subjected to the impact of the "last truth": applying the same treatment to others, and successfully, is also the means to dispel their doubts, if they have any left.

For the individual, the main consequence is the disruption of the balance between the ego and the outside world. We normally operate a constant back and forth between an experience (what comes to us from the outside world and others) and our reflection: this is how we test the reality of the environment and maintain the sense of our own identity.

However, the pressure of the totalitarian environment tends to destroy this polarity, to replace it with another: between the "real" (the ideology and the behavior of the group with which each must identify) and the "non-real" (everything else). What comes from outside is "lie." Those who manage to achieve this identification experience an exhilarating feeling of omniscience shared with the group (the Party, the People, the Leader ...); they "see the world with the eyes of God." Others feel suffocated by those who control them and will try to escape them as soon as control is relaxed (not without having consequences).

2. "Mystical manipulation"

Once environmental control has been carried out, the next inevitable step is personal manipulation. Directed "from above," it aims to provoke a set of determined behaviors and emotions, but in such a way that they are felt as spontaneous. For the manipulated, this spontaneity led by an omniscient group assumes an almost mystical quality. "I reacted according to what I had been taught." Manipulators do not only seek power over others: they too are driven by a mysticism which not only justifies but demands these manipulations. They become the instrument of their mysticism, confer a divine "aura" to manipulative institutions — Party, Government, Organization, Church. They are the agents chosen by this higher force (History, Science, God, etc.). The realization of the "mystical imperative" takes precedence over any other consideration (including immediate human well-being). Any thought or action that questions the higher goal is considered retrograde, selfish, petty. It is this mystical imperative that produces the seemingly opposite extremes of idealism and cynicism, the most cynical acts of which can be committed to serving the "supreme goal" ("the end sanctifies all means").

At the level of the individual, the answers revolve around the basic polarity between trust and distrust. He is asked to accept these manipulations based on ultimate trust — or faith — "like a child in his mother's arms," said a priest who had undergone reform in prison. Whoever experiences this degree of confidence comes to take pleasure in the suffering caused by the manipulations; he believes them necessary for the accomplishment of the "higher goal," which he has made his own. He then participates in the manipulation of others.

But such confidence is difficult to maintain permanently, and the higher goal does not always provide sufficient emotional support. The individual then responds with "pawn psychology": unable to escape from more powerful forces than him, he seeks to adapt to them above all. He develops the sense of the right answer, is sensitive to all kinds of signals, learns to anticipate the pressures of the environment, to let the wave carry himself; his psychic energies melt into the current, instead of turning against himself, which would be painful. He stops asking himself questions. For this, he must participate in the manipulation of others, bow to betrayals (towards others, and himself). His reaction can also be a mixture of the two attitudes. But anyway, he stripped himself of the ability to express himself and act independently.

3. The requirement of purity

In all situations of ideological totalitarianism, the world of experience is rigorously divided between the pure and the impure, absolute good and absolute evil. Pure and good: these are ideas, feelings, actions by the totalitarian ideology and line; everything else is relegated to the realm of the unclean and evil. Nothing human is immune to the island of moral judgments; all the "poisons," all the stains must be sought and eliminated.

The underlying assumption is that this absolute purity (the "good communist" for the Chinese ...) is possible. You can do anything in the name of this purity; it will be moral. This perfection is inaccessible, the "Reformation of thought" itself provides proof of its most malignant consequences: it creates a narrow world of guilt and shame. Ongoing reform requires everyone to strive for something that does not exist and is foreign to the human condition.

In this world, everyone should expect to be punished. As one never reaches total purity, one must expect humiliation and exclusion. The relationship with the community is a shame. Worse still: guilt and shame become values in themselves, privileged forms of communication, the subject of public competitions. Those who do not fully succeed may pretend these feelings for a while, but it's much safer to feel them.

Individuals are more or less prone to these feelings of guilt and shame, depending on their character and education, but these are universal human tendencies, and everyone is vulnerable. It is a matter of degree. The ideological totalitarianisms, setting themselves up as ultimate judges of good and evil in this world, use these tendencies as emotional levers to influence and manipulate, the individual internalizes absolute criteria and becomes his judge; but it also projects them outside: the "impurities" come from external influences. The best way to get rid of the burden of guilt is to expose these influences continually. The more guilty you feel, the greater the hatred. This leads to mass hatred, purges of heretics, to holy wars (political or religious). It is very difficult to find a more balanced sense of the complexities of human morality when one has experienced such a good-bad polarization.

4. The cult of confession

This obsession is closely linked to the requirement of absolute purity. We come to confessing imaginary crimes — this, in the hope of being healed of our sins. In the hands of totalitarians, confession becomes a means of exploiting vulnerabilities (feeling of guilt, shame) instead of relieving them.

Confession is, first of all, a means of personal purification. It is also a kind of symbolic surrender and finally, the means of maintaining total transparency vis-à-vis others, or at least the Organization, which must know all the past, the thoughts, the passions of each individual, and especially what is considered negative. This cult of confession can produce an orgiastic sense of unity between the co-confessors, a kind of ecstasy where the self merges into the great flow of the "Movement." For some, this can also satisfy a tendency to self-punishment, a desire to free oneself from repressed feelings of guilt (catharsis).

Everyone becomes a penitent judge.

5. "Sacred Science"

The totalitarian environment maintains a sacred aura around its basic dogma, presented as the ultimate moral vision for ordering human existence. It is forbidden (or impossible) to question it and implies to revere the authors of this Word and its current holders. Although this "sacred science" is in the realm of revelation, it transcends (it is superior) the ordinary rules of logic, the totalitarian environment puts an exaggerated insistence on asserting its flawless logic, its absolute "scientific" precision. Daring to criticize it, or worse, have different ideas, even unspoken, becomes not only immoral and disrespectful but "anti-scientific." We exploit here the reverence which surrounds all that is "scientific" (Especially nowadays, with advanced imaging techniques and funding allocated to research in favor of disciplines which support contemporary scientific dogma).

Here the presumption isn't that man can be God, but that man's ideas can be God — that there is an absolute science of ideas (and therefore of man) — that it can be combined with an equally absolute body of moral principles, the resulting doctrine to be true for all men at all times.

This sacred science can offer comfort and security at the level of the individual thanks to the apparent unification between the modes of mystical and logical experience. It brings together reasoning in the form of a syllogism (with a great deal of "consequently") and dazzling intuitions. The hold of this "sacred science" is so strong that the individual who feels attracted to ideas that ignore or contradict it will feel guilty and be afraid.

In a totalitarian environment, there is no distinction between the sacred and the profane. A counterfeit science mixes with a junk religion. The pressure to obtain personal closure is such that we prefer to avoid any knowledge or experience that could lead to authentic self-expression and creative evolution.

6. Coded language

In the language of the totalitarian environment, the cliché is king. The most complex human problems are reduced to a few short, peremptory sentences that are easy to remember and repeat. They are the beginning and the conclusion of all "ideological analysis." The cliché has the advantage of dispensing from any real discussion, from the exploration of various interpretations, from all personal reflection and expression.

Clichés are not only shortcuts, but they are polarized, with positive or negative emotional charges: some terms represent good, and those that represent evil, the devil. Maoist vocabulary, for example, repeated positive terms: progress, progressive, liberation, proletarian point of view, the debate of history, etc. Negative terms: capitalist, imperialist, bourgeois, exploitation... This very characteristic "language of non-thought" is frightfully boring for all those who do not share it. It also makes a member of a totalitarian group very recognizable.

Of course, every group has, to a certain extent, its jargon: family, school, profession, etc. Certain expressions are signs of recognition, but that does not prevent the members of these groups (an individual can also belong to several) from being equally at ease in general language. In the totalitarian group, the jargon becomes exclusive. It expresses the certainties of "sacred science," which strengthens them; the key expressions trigger the emotions, positive or negative, desired by the manipulators.

For the individual, this language has the effect of a narrowing ("constriction"), an impoverishment, a linguistic amputation. However, language and its richness are the very basis of human experience, and to amputate language is to remove whole swathes of the ability to think and feel, even if the individual does not realize it. Even if he takes pleasure in it, he thus feels his belonging to the group, outside of which he no longer wants to exist. It is also a very strong link with the group because the outside world becomes foreign to it. "Others don't think like we do." He even becomes a stranger to himself, to his past, to everything that made him become what he is: he can no longer even imagine his "old life" — and he does not want to: he realizes that this could constitute a danger for him.

This manipulation of language could be the subject of a special study because it is fundamental: it is the most apparent wall between the adherents of totalitarian ideology and the rest of humanity. This is often what is first felt by "the others" (those outside the totalitarian system). For Westerners leaving Chinese prisons, it was all the more obvious that their "reform" was done in Chinese; but it was equally so for the Chinese themselves. One of them said: "When we have used the same patterns of expressions for so long ... we feel chained".

7. The doctrine above the person

This sterile language also reflects the subordination of human experience to the requirements of the doctrine: personal experience, feelings are continuously channeled, put in an abstract mold of interpretation, the feelings having to correspond to the official catalog.

This is obvious in the reinterpretation of history, rewritten in the form of black and white melodrama. There too, there were the bad guys: imperialists, capitalists, foreigners, feudal reactionaries inside — and the good ones — the resistance and the liberation of the People, salvation by the victory of communism. These reinterpretations also incorporate pieces of reality, without which they would not be accepted and would remain pure mythology. The myths themselves use and reinforce existing feelings, sometimes underlying, which can be justified. All mass revolutions rewrite history, by eliminating what does not fit with doctrine, or by reinterpreting it. The history of "historians" is never entirely objective or innocent.

But a serious historian strives to disregard his preferences and prejudices; at the very least, he will clarify his point of view. But when myth merges with totalitarian "sacred science," the resulting "logic" can purely and simply eliminate and replace reality: that of historical facts, even recent ones, and individual experience.

This is how the individual remakes his past to please his masters, reinterprets his whole life, and that of his family. Character and identity must be reshaped, not by the nature and potential of each, but to sink them into the rigid mold of doctrine. Camus says that "the executioners of philosophy and state terrorism ... place an abstract concept above human life, even though they call it history, to which they would agree, subject in advance, to apply certain ideas in complete arbitrariness ...."

The assumption is that doctrine, including its mythical elements, is more valid, truer, more real than any aspect of real human character, or human experience. And if the events contradict the doctrine, we will change the events rather than the doctrine — they will be downplayed, denied, or ignored. Likewise, individuals will go so far as to agree to reinterpret their acts and attitudes to coincide with the character they become if they ever fall out of favor (if they do not have the possibility, or the strength, to get out of the totalitarian system).

8. Absolute power over existence

The totalitarian environment establishes an absolute separation between those who have the right to exist and those who do not. The latter are "non-persons"; the reform of thought provides non-persons with the means to access existence.

This sovereign right to grant or refuse existence amounts to making God: this is what the Greeks called hubris. But under this hubris, there is the conviction that there is only one way leading to the true existence, only one valid mode of existing, the totalitarian ones feel obliged to destroy all the possibilities of "false" existences: it is the means of realizing the great project of true existence, to which they are devoted. And we can consider the whole reform of thought as the means to eradicate all these modes of existence deemed false not only among non-people, but also among legitimate people, but who could be contaminated.

For the individual, it is the ultimate conflict: "to be or not to be," being or nothingness. It is also the attraction of a conversion experience which offers the only possible path to the existence. The totalitarian environment — even in the absence of physical violence — encourages everyone to fear destruction. The person can overcome this fear and find confirmation of his existence in the source of all existence that is the Totalitarian Organization.

Existence then depends on faith ("I believe, therefore I am"), submission ("I obey, therefore I am"), and, ultimately, on the feeling of total fusion with the ideological movement. Of course, everyone operates compromises and combines this dependence with elements of their own identity. But everyone is constantly reminded that the room for maneuver is narrow and that one cannot deviate much from the single path without being deprived of the right to existence.

Lifton did not determine these themes as a priori. He released them from what he had learned by listening to subjects who had undergone "thought reform." We may find that other classifications would be possible, or that certain themes overlap, at least in part. Control of the environment, that of language, and therefore of communication, are intimately linked. Any ranking is an attempt, never entirely successful, to understand the experience as much as possible.

Lifton concludes by saying that the more an environment presents these eight psychological themes, the more it resembles ideological totalitarianism. But he adds that no milieu perfectly achieves totalitarianism. Some environments, rather moderate, can manifest some. Even an environment that seems dangerously close to totalitarianism, if one base oneself on these criteria, radically differs from it, insofar as it leaves different paths open.

Totalitarianism paroxysystic experience

Totalitarianism itself can offer a "paroxysmal" experience, which makes it possible to transcend all that is ordinary, banal, to free oneself from human ambivalences, to penetrate a sphere of truth, reality, confidence, and sincerity. Beyond anything, we have ever known or imagined. However, this experience is not spontaneous but directed and manipulated. Contrary to what the great mystics, the great spirituals have known, it has the effect of closing the mind and not of greater receptivity and openness.

In the absence of paroxysmal experience, ideological totalitarianism has even more negative consequences for human potential: destructive emotions, intellectual and psychological shrinking; it deprives man of all that is the most subtle, the most imaginative — by the false promise of eliminating the imperfections, the uncertainties, and ambivalences which help to define the human condition. This is what provokes the collective excesses so characteristic of totalitarianism in all its forms. In turn, these excesses mobilize extremist tendencies among those outside who are attacked, and we enter a vicious circle.

According to Lifton, the source of ideological totalitarianism, the origin of these extreme emotional reactions is not to be found in some external evil power, but in the very depths of man: the human quest for the all-powerful guide, for supernatural force (political party, religious ideas, great leader, Science ...) capable of bringing to all men perfect solidarity, will eliminate the anxiety of death and the terror of nothingness. This quest is at the heart of all mythologies, religions, the history of all nations, as in individual life. The potential for totalitarianism is different according to societies, their history, and their structure, as individuals, according to their character, their future (family, childhood, relationships with others...). It is never absent, and we cannot predict it: two people are never identical, no more than two companies at a given time. For totalitarianism to occur, many factors must be combined, which were not all apparent or predictable.

CHAPTER 7

WHAT IS HYPNOSIS?

"I'm afraid because you're going to put me to sleep and I won't know what happened."

First of all, hypnosis is not being asleep but a modified state of consciousness. The electroencephalogram confirms this without a doubt; the tracing of a person in a hypnotic state is different from that of the sleeper. The hypnotized subjects' plots show slight changes related to suggestions, but none of the electrical signs of REM sleep or deep sleep.

James Braid, an English surgeon, is the current namer of "hypnosis." In 1855, he introduced the concept of a modified state of consciousness, which he called "the theory of hypnosis and psych corporeal healing related to a given state."

This term "hypnosis" is derived from the Greek word "hupnos" which means "sleep." This etymology is the source of misunderstandings detrimental to the current practice of this technique. Indeed, hypnosis still often evokes a mysterious, magical or disturbing sleep and this conception generates either unrealistic expectations ("I want you to put me to sleep and solve all my problems during my hypnotic sleep") or an exaggerated distrust ("You will put me to sleep and subject me without my knowledge").

Far from inducing passivity, hypnosis is an active state in which several phenomena occur through your collaboration. No practitioner can induce you into a hypnotic state if you don't want to. To make a comparison, you may be required to go to the cinema but not to watch the film. Indeed, to not see, you just close your eyes.

Hypnosis, therefore, requires your participation. You will remain present and witness what is happening inside you, even in a deep trance. While one part of you will be engaged in hypnotic work, another will remain in the observer position. For example, you can relive memories and the different sensations associated with it while remaining aware of the hypnotic context of reviviscency. The hypnotic trance can be compared to the viewer's state of attention fully captivated by a thriller. This one does not sleep, and the film absorbs him to the point of disinteresting the world around him (it is "in" the film, he is "in") but keeps in mind that he is in a movie theatre.

Also, be aware that you will only agree to respond to suggestions if they are consistent with your core values.

"If it's not sleeping, what is hypnosis?"

It is essentially a state of mental concentration during which the faculties of the person's mind are so overwhelmed by an idea, internal images, sensations, or emotions that he is momentarily indifferent to most aspects of external reality. If certain psychic functions are dormant, it is for the benefit of other processes, especially unconscious.

In hypnosis, our perceptions and understanding of reality are altered, allowing us to function mentally in a different way and to be more open to ourselves. However, during the first sessions of hypnosis, it often happens that the patient does not feel like he is having a particular experience and will need some learning to access deeper states. However, it should be noted that the depth of the trance is not necessarily a criterion of quality. Surprising therapeutic results can be seen as a result of superficial hypnotic experiments. Psychological work can be compared to swimming. You can swim both in the small and in the great depth of a swimming pool. Similarly, quality work can be done both in a light trance and in a deep hypnotic state.

"Hypnosis is an unusual, abnormal, and artificial condition."

No, quite the opposite. Hypnosis is a common physiological condition that we all know.

If you are a motorist, you will have noticed that when you are focused on a subject of concern to you, you can drive automatically and not notice how far you have come. Similarly, you may have already experienced a second condition called "Highway hypnosis" when you drive alone in a silent atmosphere on a tree-lined road. If you're a film buff or a literature buff, you've probably been so "caught" in a story that you don't hear what a person is saying to you. You know how easy it is to forget the time that passes if you're passionate about computer science or video games. You also certainly "unhooked" from the outside reality in a waiting room or in a station hall to absorb you into yourself.

In all these situations, you have experienced an "ordinary daily trance." These states have, in common, a spontaneous shift of our attention to internal stimuli. We go through this type of hypnotic state, every day, every 90 to 100 minutes. These common trances are linked to the ultradian cycle, which also rhythms other physiological parameters. During these phases, some parts of our brain rest while others are activated, allowing a different functioning necessary for the mental organization of information and lived experiences.

In a schematic way, and with all the reservations imposed by this simplification, there would be, in a trance, a departmentalization of the left brain and activation of the right hemisphere.

According to neurophysiological theories, each of the cerebral hemispheres brings a different understanding of reality. The left brain would dominate the awakening activities, while the right brain would manifest itself mainly during dreaming, daydreaming, artistic activity, common trance, and hypnosis. With this in mind, it is accepted that the right hemisphere is responsible for unconscious phenomena and that it has greater activity when the usual consciousness is altered.

The state of hypnosis is, therefore, a natural and banal physiological phenomenon, and therapeutic hypnosis is only the amplification of this phenomenon with the help of another person.

"With me, it's not going to work because I have a strong character, or only the weak can be hypnotized."

Given what has just been mentioned, it seems obvious that each of us is capable of experiencing satisfying hypnotic states to varying degrees.

Hypnotism would be a relatively stable psychological data that would depend on the hypnotized and not the hypnotist. According to research, it is linked in particular to intelligence and the capacity of the imagination. So, you have all the more assets to start hypnotherapy as you have character!

You will have to learn not to do anything, to forget the outside world temporarily, and to let go. To the extent that we are used to being vigilant, learning a new type of behavior is a difficult matter.

"I don't want to lose control! I don't want to be under the power of the hypnotist!"

During the hypnosis sessions, the hypnotist tends to make it seem that he is the custodian of exceptional power to make a spectator do anything. This hypnotic power is a decoy. On the other hand, it is a real power of intellectual manipulation! In reality, no hypnotist can force you to execute or say things you don't want.

You will be the only one behind your altered states of consciousness. You will have control over your behaviour throughout the session. The therapist is only an instrument that, thanks to his know-how, will help you to emerge a process that you will keep in control of. You will learn to let go by immediately regaining control of operations. Therapeutic hypnosis is not intended to subject you, but rather to increase your control over yourself.

It may be surprising, at first glance, that this state of letting go is an opportunity for better personal control.

Neurophysiological data can help to understand this phenomenon. Many psychological problems could be understood, such as the misapplication of rational approaches in the left hemisphere on situations that would be better understood by the right brain. Right brain stimulant hypnosis would, therefore, help the subject solve his difficulties through his solutions. Indeed, the latter already has the necessary resources in him, but he ignores them because they are outside his usual consciousness.

The hypnotherapist, it will be understood, is not intended to impose his solutions but to explore your unsuspected and unused potentialities with you. In this modified state of consciousness, you will start new solutions using the therapist's words and images that are relevant to you.

Here, if it were still needed, one last proof, by the absurd, of the inconsistency of this myth of the almighty hypnotist: it is possible to induce oneself a hypnotic state by resorting to his suggestions. This is called self-hypnosis. We have evoked the fact that we experience altered states of consciousness in our daily lives. These are of a self-hypnosis type. Therapeutic self-hypnosis is only the structured use of this phenomenon. We can, therefore, say that hypnosis is always in the essence of self-hypnosis and that even when a therapist is called upon, the therapist only guides the patient to trance.

"I'm afraid hypnosis is dangerous and harmful."

This widespread belief is false, with some reservations. Indeed, if hypnosis did not pose any danger, its beneficial action could be questioned. The risk of creating psychosomatic or psychiatric disorders exists, although these are rare and transient.

Negative self-hypnosis is used to describe a negative self-perception that causes pathogenic unconscious processes to start. Negative thoughts that the subject would have located himself outside his usual consciousness and beyond criticism would be powerful suggestions. According to the author, these self-suggestions are responsible for many disorders, including sexual disorders.

Moreover, psycho-neuro-immunology teaches us that the mind, through emotions and mental attitudes, can play a significant role in the genesis of bodily dysfunction or disease.

It cannot, therefore, be completely rejected, the assumption that a suggestion made by a hypnotist to a subject in modified consciousness cannot act negatively on him, either physically or psychologically. However, it is clear that the harmful consequences of hypnosis only appear in people with a long medical history and who have previously exhibited psychotic tendencies.

Hypnosis is, in fact, no more or less dangerous than any other form of the psychotherapeutic relationship. After prior interviews, practiced by a qualified professional, who remains in his usual therapeutic framework, it is, on the contrary, an extraordinary tool. Indeed, the hypnotic state offers the patient an experience during which the usual limitations of his thoughts are temporarily suspended.

Beliefs, habits, and preconceived ideas accepted since childhood can block opportunities for development or adaptation. However, these difficult borders to cross in the usual waking state are erased during trance, and returns in the apprehension of reality become possible. In other words, in hypnosis, the perception of what we are experiencing is changed, allowing us to be more open to ourselves and to change.

Let us define hypnosis proposed by the British Medical Association: "transient state of modified attention in the subject, a condition that can be produced by another person and in which various phenomena may appear spontaneously or in response to verbal or other stimuli. These phenomena include a change in consciousness and memory, increased susceptibility to suggestion, and the appearance in the subject of answers and ideas that are not familiar to him in his usual state of mind. Also, phenomena such as anaesthesia, paralysis, muscle rigidity, and vasomotor modifications can be, in the hypnotic state, produced and suppressed."

Sensory alterations are a usual phenomenon

The most common are heaviness or numbness in the body (especially the limbs), feelings of flutter or lightness, feelings of warmth or freshness, the feeling that the volume of the body changes (usually, the hands or feet), loss of sensation of limb positioning (for example, patients no longer feel / no longer know how their hands are placed), anesthesia and analgesia.

Time distortion. It is a change in the perception of the length of time that elapses. For example, the patient may feel that the session has been longer or, on the contrary, shorter than it has objectively been.

Post-hypnotic amnesia. Sometimes the patient forgets what happened during part or all of the hypnosis session.

Hypermnesia. It allows you to find memories, consciously forgotten. However, if hypnosis allows you to recover elements of the past, it can also create false memories. This ability to modify memory is also used therapeutically, in particular to create repairing scenarios.

Other frequent small signs include tearing and difficulty in speech.

Not everyone can realize all of these phenomena. Everyone can be gifted for some and not others, but hypnosis more often than not allows you to learn or cultivate them. Each of these signs can have therapeutic dimensions.

The actual induction of the hypnotic state

To enter a trance, you don't have to be fascinated by the look of a magician. The patient does not enter a trance because the hypnotist imposes it but because he wants it.

Induction is nothing more than a technique that helps the patient enter a state of inner focus.

The methods of induction of the hypnotic state are very numerous. They have in common to focus attention on an object (an object that the patient freely chooses in the room, across or a dot drawn on one of his hands, etc.), physical sensations (for example, the progressive heaviness of the body or breathing) or mental images (for example, a memory). One can practice an induction by relaxation with an awareness of bodily sensations or accompaniment in a pleasant memory. These are simple and often effective ways of doing things. The person is asked to concentrate as much as possible to make the memory more and more vivid. To do this, the hypnotist helps him to see, hear, and feel the different aspects of the situation. He absorbs himself so that he forgets what surrounds him. The usual conscious mind "picks up," and the unconscious emerges.

The inductions of the first hypnotic states are, on average, about fifteen minutes. However, this duration is most often significantly reduced as the sessions go on.

Therapeutic work in hypnosis

Since the hypnotic state is induced, therapeutic ideas will be presented to patients through suggestions and metaphors.

Suggestions are ways of proposing creative solutions to the patient's problem. In Ericksonian hypnosis, unlike traditional hypnosis, the suggestion is not an order but rather "an opportunity to make a new experience in an attitude of availability" (Godin). To suggest something to a person is not to condemn them to obey it. A suggestion is only a suggestion, and the unconscious of the subject is free to refuse or accept it, in part or totally. The therapist's goal is not to instill in the patient any well-made solutions, but to enable the patient to develop his internal skills.

Metaphors are stories, tales, anecdotes bearing an apparent meaning that captures conscious attention and a hidden meaning proposing solutions to the patient's problem.

The action of suggestions and metaphors is the result of a psychological process called ideodynamicism. This natural phenomenon activates ideas to turn into an act or sensation (as the evocation of a lemon in the mouth can cause salivation).

In some cases, the therapist may conduct interactive sessions in which the patient's unconscious will be "questioned" or directly mobilized to solve a specific problem. Without wanting to be exhaustive, we can mention the technique of the affect bridge, and that of the somatic bridge used respectively to know the origin of a psychological problem and an organic disease. Some painful memories can be the subject of a restorative scenario. The therapist will help the patient to relive the painful scenes in hypnosis and transform them so that he can experience them with the resources he then lacked. We should also mention the regression in age, useful to find problematic moments of the past and progression in the future that helps the patient to project himself into a future free of the problem. However, it should be noted that this session requires an experienced therapist and that the patient has access to good quality trance.

The termination phase and the exit from the hypnotic state.

The completion of hypnosis is gradual. The actual exit from

the hypnotic state will be preceded by a latency during which the practitioner will make positive post-hypnotic suggestions for relaxation and well-being. The therapist will then accompany the "wake-up call" by counting and asking the patient to go back to each figure stated gradually.

Post-hypnotic interview

Care will be taken to allow the person to narrate his experience from the trance, and this for at least two reasons. The first is that the person will give information that will allow the therapist to adapt his techniques as best as possible during the later sessions. The second reason is that during these interviews, the patient gives crucial indications about his psychology. However, hypnosis is a therapy in its own right and, as such, cannot worry about the symptom without worrying about the rest.

CHAPTER 8

PSYCHOANALYSIS TECHNIQUES OF SIGMUND FREUD

In this chapter, we are going to examine carefully some questions that interest the theory, several topics that affect the technique, and a few issues that concern the clinic around which psychoanalysis takes on its entity. But before starting this, it is necessary to place this particular therapeutic method in its conceptual dimension. Psychoanalysis is a treatment of a psychological nature that takes place between a specialist and a person who needs help due to their emotional problems. "It is carried out by a systematized methodology and based on certain theoretical foundations, and its purpose is to eliminate or diminish the suffering and behavioral disorders derived from such alterations, through the interpersonal relationship between the therapist and the patient."

Unfortunately, and despite such laudable ends, psychoanalysis has carried unwanted connotations throughout its history. Some of them have referred to their fundamentally mentalistic character, others to their excessive medical dependence, and, some more, to their marked unscientific condition. Mentalists, for being based conceptually on constructs about the psychic apparatus and intrapsychic conflict, little accessible to observation. Medical, for having been in its origins an almost exclusive professional domain of the medical professional.

Unscientific in that the analysis process cannot be described operationally and unrepeatable, almost irreplaceable experiences are managed. These and other peculiarities have contributed to psychoanalysis being considered more as a practice than as an applied scientific discipline.

Definition of Psychoanalysis

Before going on to point out the fundamental aspects that psychoanalysis contributes to modern psychotherapy, it is necessary to remember, even briefly, the beginnings of scientific psychotherapy and the current conceptions among S. Freud's contemporaries, to show more clearly the dimension and importance of psychoanalytic contributions. For this reason, we want to begin by outlining our way of understanding Freud's work and our particular point of view on psychoanalysis as a therapeutic method. Quoting Freud more or less extensively serves several causes. The most important of them is that, despite some excellent attempts at systematization, today, the statement is that "the best way to understand psychoanalysis is to follow the trajectory of its genesis and its evolution." The assimilation of classical texts remains a prerequisite to be able to understand the current problems of psychoanalysis and to be able to find more adequate solutions to modern times.

With this original intention, on the other hand, we want to meet the sources that have fed the therapeutic aspect of psychoanalysis. For this reason, too, we try to make the passages we quote serve as support and justification for our opinions in the process of argumentative interaction with

Freud himself. Using quotes and examples that determine and demonstrate which have been the lines of development that have led us from the origins of psychoanalysis to current intervention strategies, we aim to achieve a systematic description of psychoanalysis historically oriented. Why do we proceed in this way? Because, undoubtedly, the divergences and contradictions that appear in Freud's work, as well as its variations over the decades, testify to the opening of psychoanalysis, which "scores without leaving the support of experienced, is always considered unfinished, and he is always ready to rectify or replace his theories."

Since his Psychology Project (1895), Freud cherished the idea of integrating all his discoveries into the general body of science, just as it was conceived in his time. For this reason, when I had to describe and explain what else was psychoanalysis, underlining once again the inseparable bond between cure and research, he did not hesitate to define it as follows:

Psychoanalysis is the name:

1) Of a procedure for the investigation of mental processes more or less inaccessible by another means.

2) Of a method based on this research for the treatment of neurotic disorders.

3) A series of psychological conceptions acquired by this means and that progressively converge to form a new discipline.

This definition, which appeared in his article Psychoanalysis and Libido Theory, is frequently cited because it delimits what the great ones must be psychoanalysis problems. Let us analyze, then, each one of the sections of this definition:

a) For Freud, psychoanalysis is a research method that leads to the discovery and knowledge of new psychological facts that are hardly accessible by any other means. From this point of view, Freud was separated from philosophy and said so, and viewed its creation as a branch of psychology and as a part of science. He said that science consists of the formulation of hypotheses that lead to observation, which brings order and clarity to the phenomena studied. In love with his method and amazed at the importance of his discoveries, he felt the need for tight and precise definitions, but he had to accept, not without qualms, during the early stages of certain science, aspects of vagueness in concepts and a certain degree of speculation in theories.

"The true principle of scientific activity consists rather in the description of phenomena, which are then grouped, ordered, and related to each other ... Only after having further developed the research in the field in question will we be able to formulate scientific concepts that make it up more clearly. Thus, we can gradually modify these concepts until they become widely applicable and, at the same time, acquire logical consistency".

This is why the claim of experimental verification of psychoanalytic facts using techniques derived from other research methods is so problematic. It is not that there can be no verification but that it is very difficult to carry out with other methods. Therefore, Rosenzweig wrote to Freud to explain the experimental results of the validation tests to which he had submitted some psychoanalytic concepts. He replied that "the psychoanalytic concepts were based on reliable and abundant observations and therefore did not need independent experimental verification. Attitudes like this did not favor the understanding or acceptance of those who studied the same field, although with different perspectives.

b) In the second section of the definition, an implicit reference is made to the therapeutic nature of psychoanalysis and, therefore, to the clinic. Although for some psychoanalysis is an occupation of aesthetes and dilettants, the clinical spirit constitutes the best defense against analytical academicism that tends, in its theorizing zeal, to replace concrete drama with a conflict of abstract entities. The clinical observation of the patient's behaviors is what suggests the hypothesis and allows its verification. The behavioral clinic is the one that proposes the therapy, controls its progress, and diagnoses the cure.

Thus, defining psychoanalysis as "the exploration of the unconscious " is insufficient. As Lagache (1969) rightly points out, a definition of psychoanalysis cannot be attempted by excluding it from the framework of clinical psychology of human behavior, the more specific character of which would be the attention it gives to transference. However, there is no doubt that there are discrepancies among analysts themselves about the scope and meaning of the term psychoanalysis, as well as controversies regarding the types of contracts and the different frameworks and rhythms of work. There is a discrepancy, for example, about disorders accessible to psychoanalysis. Some contemporary psychoanalysts have been interested in the extension or application of psychoanalysis outside the field of neuroses. But other psychoanalysts ridicule his performance since they are convinced that those who decide to delve into the indecipherable world of psychoses, unfortunately, have launched into a company that falls outside the analytical task: "to use the technique that Freud instituted outside of the experience to which it is applied is to row when the boat is in the sand" (J. Lacan, quoted by Laplanche, 1974). In any case, and without going into the legitimacy of these positions, in our opinion, this is not the case, as evidenced by the abundant current literature on the treatment of psychosis, perversions, psychosomatic disorders, etc.

c) The third point of the definition ensures that psychoanalysis is a science. Throughout all his work, the reasons and arguments that Freud uses to underline the scientific nature of his investigations multiply. Even with all the doubts and hesitations that may arise in someone who is only beginning to glimpse the vast possibilities offered by his research method, the creator of psychoanalysis was fully convinced of the suitability and truthfulness of his hypotheses that, in daily practice from the clinic, they were shown to him as undoubtedly plausible. So much so that, since his Psychology Project (1895), Freud always cherished the idea of integrating the set of his discoveries in the general body of science, at least, as they were conceived in his time. No doubt for Freud, the psychoanalytic method created a "New scientific discipline."

In his opinion, when analyzing a patient's psychoanalysis works scientifically, try to put your expectations aside and embrace patient data as it arises. He collects many disparate pieces of the patient's speech, pieces that seem not to match each other, and establishes laws to order and organize such disparate data. These laws or rules are contrasted with subsequent observations made during the analysis. Furthermore, the observations obtained from one patient are contrasted with those of another patient, and the observations of one analyst are contrasted with those of other analysts. As if this were not enough, the work's observations with the patients are in contrast with cultural documents, such as myths, legends, artistic material or folk customs, rituals, religious beliefs, etc. Even as Pervin (1979) points out, psychoanalytic hypotheses can be contrasted with observations extracted from psychological tests administered on a large scale.

It is clear, then, that this research method allows obtaining a large amount of data about a subject. There is possibly no other psychology procedure that does not even come close to the wealth of material obtained from a single person by the psychoanalyst. However, the analyst, unlike other scientists, does not carry out experiments — Freud himself pointed out. This is the great obstacle, the great pending subject, that psychoanalysis has to face. However, this great gap between experimentality and psychoanalysis has been narrowing to the extent that, in the last thirty years, some researchers have directed their interest towards psychoanalysis. Some analysts have tried to validate certain contents of the theory empirically.

Unfortunately, despite this approach of positions and these attempts at empirical validation, the claim that psychoanalysis is a natural science is not endorsed by all analysts. There is a current of thought within psychoanalysis, also supported by some non-psychoanalytic philosophers such as P. Ricoeur (1970) and J. Habermas (1971), who considers that psychoanalysis does not belong at all to the natural sciences, but is a science interpretive, in Ricoeur's words, a hermeneutic. In J. Blight's (1981) opinion, this renunciation of psychoanalysis as science has its origin in the publication of the proceedings of the symposium led by S. Hook, a symposium intended to discuss the place that corresponds to psychoanalysis within the world of science. (Hook 1959, Nagel 1959). From this event, a significant number of psychoanalysts decided that it was not worth the effort to find arguments that refute the criticisms that psychoanalysis was receiving and that it was unnecessary to seek new forms of research with which to validate or refute, psychoanalytic hypotheses, in order to accredit psychoanalysis as a scientific method.

To the question, Freud asks himself in Some Elementary Lessons on Psychoanalysis (1940) about what else psychoanalysis can be if it is not a science. They answered that psychoanalysis was something different from natural science; it was a hermeneutical science. These authors, and others with them, maintain that Freudian metapsychology, which tries to explain the causes of psychic processes, is like a foreign body in the psychoanalytic building that must be eliminated. Starting from the basis that two theories coexist in psychoanalysis, the clinical-psychological theory, which seeks to interpret the reasons and motives for human behavior — that is, to understand — and the metapsychological theory, which seeks to delimit and define the causes of This behavior — that is to say, explain — carried out what Blight calls an "atherectomy," an amputation of one of the theories, the metapsychological one, considering that it was nothing more than an erroneous sample of Freud's fidelity to the positivism of his time.

In summary, then, we can say that in psychoanalysis, despite these theoretical discrepancies, there has always been an inseparable union between healing and research, knowledge brought success, and it was not possible to try without finding something new, nor did you gain clarification without experiencing its therapeutic effect. "Our analytical procedure is the only one in which this precious conjunction remains assured. Only if we practice our analytical spiritual guide will we be able to deepen our developing conception of the human mind.

The Psychoanalysis Technique

For historians, López Piñero and Morales Meseguer (1970), psychotherapy in the strict sense did not appear until the middle years of the 19th century, when a series of British doctors, WB Carpenter and DH Tuke especially, began to think of new ideas about the relations between the body and the mind and regarding hypnotic techniques since hypnotism made possible the investigation of automatic, unconscious processes and the relation body-mind. However, it was James Braid (1795-1860), a prestigious Scottish surgeon, who took the decisive step from animal magnetism to "nervous sleep" or hypnosis. Despite all the criticism, Braid immediately grasped the healing possibilities of the hypnotic procedure, and in 1843 he risked publishing his seminal work, Neurypnology, where he exposes his method and the properties of the hypnotic state.

Hypnotism was welcomed by some British authors as a therapeutic hope, a progress that could generate changes in the patient's diseases, but the main thing is that these initial works were not isolated, but had a great influence on the evolution of French psychotherapy. Indeed, from 1860 the French became interested in the subject of "nervous sleep." This was the year in which Liébeault began the practice of hypnotism, and shortly afterward, Théodule Ribot (1839-1916) introduced texts on English and German positive psychology in France. This growing interest in hypnotism led to the emergence of two important schools in France that, at the same time that they studied the subject of hypnosis, advanced in the clinical care of neurotics.

Thus, as Horacio Etchegoyen (1986) suggests, it can be said that psychoanalysis is undoubtedly a special form of psychotherapy. Psychotherapy begins to be considered scientific in nineteenth-century France. The two were founded and developed great schools on the suggestion that we have already mentioned in the previous chapter, one of them in Nancy, with Liébeault and Bernheim, and the other in Salpêtrière, with Jean-Martin Charcot. Precisely, the rivalry between the two schools — Charcot thought that hypnosis, far from being a method of curing diseases, was something related to hysterics, and at the same time, Liébeault argued that hypnosis was a normal phenomenon that could be induced in most people — mark the 1880s to 1890s. This statement can certainly be disputed, but there is no doubt that the climate of research on hysteria and hypnosis in France greatly influenced the young Sigmund Freud.

For what we have just said, and without wishing to review its history again, the birth of psychotherapy can be linked to France in the mid-nineteenth century. When Auguste Ambroise Liébeault turns his humble rural practice into the most important hypnotism research center in the world, this ancient technique, which twenty years before had received a name and endorsement from Braid, begins to be applied, at the same time, as an instrument of research and as a therapeutic technique. Liébeault uses it to show "the influence of morality on the body" and to "cure the sick"; the importance of their work is such that many authors do not hesitate to locate the beginning of psychotherapy in Nancy.

We will accept this statement with a single objection. The hypnotic treatment that Liébeault inaugurates is, without a doubt, personal and direct. Message and drug at the same time, are addressed to the psyche of the patient with the evident intention of curing him. Truthfully, there is still something missing to be psychotherapy: the patient receives the doctor's curative influence in a passive attitude. He does not actively and dynamically participate in the process. From a demanding point of view, the treatment used in Nancy's school is personal, but not interpersonal. Only when H. Bernheim, following the lines of Liébeault's research, places increasing emphasis on suggestion as to the source of the hypnotic and motor effect of human behavior, does the doctor-patient interaction emerge as one of the defining characteristics of the psychotherapy.

In his New Studies (1891), Bernheim reveals the amazing value of suggestion as a therapeutic agent in the treatment of hysteria, showing that the relationship between the hypnotized and the hypnotist is one of the cornerstones that support this particular type of intervention. Shortly afterward, the works of P. Janet in Paris and J. Breuer and S. Freud in Vienna, where the interpersonal relationship is increasingly evident and forced, partially give reason to these first intuitions of the School from Nancy. When Janet and Freud tried to cure the rich hysterical symptoms, they realized, each on their own, the enormous importance that some psychic aspects had in this pathology that went beyond the space of consciousness (unconscious) and that therefore, the therapist-patient relationship had to be necessarily one of the fundamental axes of any type of psychotherapy. From this moment, any treatment aimed at the patient's psyche will be considered as psychotherapy, in a framework of interpersonal relationship, and supported by a scientific theory of personality.

As Etchegoyen (1986) rightly points out, Freud psychotherapy has some characteristic features that stand out for its historical evolution. Through its method, psychotherapy addresses the psyche through the only practicable way: communication, whose instrument is the word (or rather verbal and pre-verbal language). Message and drug at the same time; its framework is the therapist-patient interpersonal relationship. And finally, its purpose is to heal, and any communication process that does not have that purpose (teaching, indoctrination, etc.) will never be psychotherapy.

However, as the scientific methods of suggestive and hypnotic psychotherapy reach their maximum development, a new line of research begins that must operate a Copernican turn in the theory and practice of psychotherapy. Towards 1880, Joseph Breuer (1842-1925), applying the hypnotic technique to a patient who, in the annals of our discipline, was named Anna O. (and whose real name was Bertha Pappenheim), found himself practicing a radically different form of psychotherapy.

Freud's new technique: Psychoanalysis

From what has been said so far, we can consider that the therapeutic method practiced by Freud and known by the name of psychoanalysis has its point starting in the cathartic procedure, whose description has been detailed by J. Breuer and Freud himself in work published jointly by them under the title of Studies on hysteria (1895). Cathartic therapy was a discovery by Breuer, who had obtained, ten years before, the cure of a hysterical woman, in whose treatment she also came to glimpse the pathogenesis of the symptoms that the patient presented. The cathartic procedure had as its main premise that the patient was hypnotizable. Its effectiveness rested fundamentally on the expansion of the field of consciousness that took place during the hypnotic trance. The hypnotized memories, ideas, and impulses that had been absent until then in her consciousness emerged. Once the subject communicated to the doctor, between intense affective manifestations, such emotional processes, the symptoms were overcome, and their reappearance was avoided.

However, this simple therapeutic intervention scheme was complicated in almost all cases, as it turned out that a single traumatic impression was not usually involved in the genesis of the symptom, but rather that a good number of them were usually associated with the symptom. Furthermore, Freud always declared himself a bad hypnotist, perhaps because it was true or because, in reality, the cathartic method did not satisfy his scientific curiosity. And that was how he decided to abandon hypnosis and develop a new technique that would help him to get to the essence of trauma, a technique more in line with his idea of the psychological reason for wanting to forget the traumatic event. In any case, if the cathartic method had given up suggestions, Freud went one step further and gave up hypnosis.

He dared to take this bold step by recalling a famous experience of post-hypnotic suggestion, carried out by Bernheim, which he had to witness during his stay at the clinic in Nancy. When the experimenter gave a person a hypnotic trance to do something after awakening, the order was carried out exactly, and the author could not explain the reason for his actions and appealed to trivial explanations. However, if the investigator did not comply with these rationalizations (as E. Jones would call them many years later), the subject ended up remembering the order received when he was in a trance. And on this basis, he changed his technique: instead of hypnotizing his patients, he began to stimulate them, to invite them to remember.

This is how Freud operated with Miss Lucy and especially with Elisabeth von R., and this new technique, associative coercion, confronted him with new facts that would have to modify his theories again. Associative coercion confirmed to Freud that things are forgotten when you do not want to remember them. You do not want to remember them because they are painful, ugly, and unpleasant, contrary to ethics and aesthetics. This process of repression, this selective forgetfulness, was reproduced before his eyes in treatment, and then he found that his patients did not want to remember, that there was a force that opposed the memory. This is how Freud discovers resistance, the cornerstone of psychoanalysis. What at the moment of trauma conditioned forgetfulness is what at this moment, in treatment, conditions resistance: there is a play of forces, a conflict between the desire to remember and the desire to forget. And if this is so, then coercion is no longer justified, because you will always stumble upon resistance. Better to let the patient speak, to speak freely. In this curious way, a new theory, the theory of resistance, leads to a new technique: Free Association, typical of psychoanalysis, which is introduced as a technical precept, as a fundamental rule.

With this newly created technical instrument, new and surprising facts will be discovered, against which the theory of trauma and pathogenic memory gradually gives way to sexual theory. Conflict, for example, is no longer a matter that concerns only the will to remember and the desire to forget. On the contrary, there is now a tendency to interpret conflict as a problem between mechanical forces and repressive forces. From this moment on, the findings multiply infantile sexuality and the Oedipus complex, the unconscious with its laws and its contents, the theory of transfer, etc. It is a new context of great discoveries in which interpretation appears as the fundamental technical instrument. When it was just a matter of retrieving a memory, neither the cathartic method nor the associative coercion required interpretation. Now everything is different, and now the subject has to be given precise reports about himself and what is happening to him so that he can better understand his psychological reality, that is, that this revealing action must be carried out by force. In psychoanalysis, it is called interpreting.

In other words, in the first decade of the century, the theory of resistance expanded vigorously in two directions: on the one hand, the unconscious (the resisted) was discovered with its laws (condensation, displacement) and its contents (libido theory), and on the other hand, the theory of transfer emerges, a precise way of defining the doctor-patient relationship. Indeed, the first glimpses of the discovery of transference are found in the Studies on Hysteria (1895). In Dora's epilogue, written in January 1901 and published in 1905, the phenomenon of transference is already practically completely deciphered. It is precisely from that moment when the new theory begins to influence the technique and imprints its Councils to the doctor (1912) and on the initiation of treatment (1913), contemporary works on the dynamics of transfer.

The immediate repercussion of transfer theory on technique is a reformulation of the analytical relationship, which from now on, will be defined in precise and rigorous terms. The frame, we will see, is nothing more than the technical response to what Freud had understood in the clinic about the peculiar relationship of the analyst and his analysand. The belle époque of the technique in which the famous Man of Rats was invited to tea and herring has been definitively closed. For the transference to emerge clearly and the patient to be properly analyzed, Freud said in 1912, the analyst must take the place of a mirror that only reflects what is shown to him.

In any case, the coherence between theory and technique is understood at this point. The doctor must show nothing of himself: without letting himself be wrapped in the nets of the transfer, he will simply return to the patient what he has placed on the smooth mirror of his technique. For this reason, Freud (1915) says, study the love of transference, that the analysis must be developed in abstinence, which sanctions the substantial change of the technique in the second decade of the century. If there were no transference theory, there would be no reason for this advice to be entirely unnecessary in the cathartic method or the primitive psychoanalysis of associative coercion. Here again, we see this unique interaction between theory and technique that we point out as specific to psychoanalysis.

On the other hand, if we have discussed transfer theory in some detail here, it is because it clearly illustrates the thesis we are developing. As Freud becomes aware of the transference, its intensity, its complexity, and its spontaneity (although this is still being discussed today), a radical change in the frame is imposed on him. The lax framing of the Rat Man, which included tea, sandwiches, and herrings, is made more rigorous by the theory of transference, a fact that in turn allows greater precision in the appreciation of the transference phenomenon as long as that a stricter and more stable framing avoids the possible manipulations of the participants and makes it sharper, more transparent.

The Interpretation Of Dreams

"If I cannot reconcile the heavenly gods, I will move those of hell."

Already in the preface to the first edition of the

Interpretation of Dreams (1900), Freud refers to the dream phenomenon as the first link in a series of abnormal psychic manifestations that interest the doctor for practical reasons, since for whoever fails to understand and explain the genesis of dream images, it will be difficult to understand the nature of phobias, obsessive ideas or delusions, and much less will they be able to exert a possible therapeutic influence on such pathologies. Furthermore, he is convinced that he can demonstrate the existence of a psychological technique that allows us to interpret dreams: psychoanalysis, a technique thanks to which each dream is revealed as "a psychic product full of meaning, to which it can be assigned a perfectly determined place in the soul activity of the awakened life."

Encouraged by this conviction, Freud carries out an exhaustive examination of the literature existing up to that time on dreams and the scientific status of dream problems, trying to clarify the processes on which the "singular and impenetrable appearance of dreams" depends — and trying to deduce from these processes a reliable conclusion about the nature of those psychic forces from whose joint or opposite action the dream phenomenon arises. The difficulty of writing a history of our scientific knowledge of dream phenomena is enormous, since, despite the efforts of many authors, it has not been possible to establish a firm base of indisputable results on which other researchers could continue building. Still, each author has started anew, and from the beginning, the study of the same phenomena.

The people of classical antiquity, for example, admitted that dreams were about the world of superhuman beings of their mythology and brought with them divine or demonic revelations, also possessing a certain intention regarding the subject: to announce the future. In the two studies that Aristotle dedicates to this matter, on the contrary, dreams appear as a much more human question: they are not divine, but demonic since Nature is demonic and not divine. To put it another way, dreams do not correspond to a supernatural revelation but obey the laws of our human spirit, although later, this spirit is closely related to divinity. Dreams are thus defined as "the mental activity of the sleeper during the resting state."

It would be wrong, however, to suppose that the theory of the supernatural origin of dreams already lacks supporters at present. On the contrary, we still find "men of subtle ingenuity," and inclined to everything extraordinary, who try to support the insolubility of dream enigma and religious faith in the existence and intervention of superhuman spiritual forces. For this reason, and since it has not been possible to analyze and master all the existing literature on this matter, Freud prefers to adapt his exposition on dreams to the themes and not to the authors, indicating in the study of each one of the dream enigmas the material that we can find for the solution of the same in previous works and authors. Let's discuss some of these puzzles below:

1. Relationship of sleep with awake life. Regarding this dream enigma, and in light of the literature that he has been able to handle, Freud raises the existence of two opposed positions. On the one hand, that defended by the old physiologist Burdach, to whom we owe a conscientious description of dreamlike phenomena, which states that "daytime life, with its works and pleasures, its joys and sorrows, is never repeated; on the contrary, the dream tends to free us from it. Even in those moments in which our whole soul is saturated by an object, in which a deep pain tears our inner life, or a work monopolizes all our spiritual forces, the dream gives us something alien to our situation; it only takes significant fragments of reality for its combinations, or it merely acquires the tone of our state of mind and symbolizes real circumstances" (OC p. 352). On the other hand, the one that gathers the widespread conviction that most dreams, despite their apparent singularity, lead us back to ordinary life instead of freeing ourselves from it. Jessen affirms in his Psychology (1855), "to a greater or lesser degree, the content of dreams is always determined by the individual personality, by age, sex, position, degree of culture and gender of the routine life of the subject, and by the events and teachings of his past. For his part, Freud openly declares himself in favor of this second option, resorting to the theories of FW Hildebrandt (1875) on the dream to justify his position:

"However unique their formations may be, they cannot become independent from the real world, and all their creations, both the most sublime and the most ridiculous, must always take their fundamental theme from what in the sensory world has appeared before our eyes or has found in any way a place of our waking thought; that it is, from what we have already lived before exterior or interior mind.

2. The dream material. Memory in the dream. There is no doubt that most of the material that makes up the content of the dream comes from what is lived and is, therefore, reproduced — remembered — in the dream. However, it would be a mistake to suppose that a mere comparison between the content of the dream and the events of awakened life is sufficient to show the relationship between them. On the contrary, only after painstaking and careful observation and analysis did we discover their links, and even, in some cases, managed to remain hidden for a long time. We observe, first of all, that in the content of the dream appears a material that later, in the awakened life, is not recognized as belonging to our knowledge or our experience. We remember, of course, that we have dreamed of this or that occurrence, but we do not remember ever having lived it. We are surprised and puzzled by the content of our dreams, being unable to explain from what source the dream has taken its components and in what subtle way they have become integrated. Despite this not very encouraging panorama, Freud seems to be very clear about things:

a) One of the sources from which the dream extracts the material it reproduces is the child's life, the childhood of the individual.

b) Elements can be discovered in dreams (people, objects, places, events, etc.) that correspond to experiences lived in the immediately preceding days, what Freud calls "day remains".

c) In the selection of the material that we reproduce in dreams, it is not always the most important thing that is taken into account, as happens in the awake life, but the most indifferent and trivial.

3. Stimuli and sources of dreams. The discussion about the provoking causes of dreams has always occupied a prominent place in dream literature. Whether the provocative stimulus of dreams was always the same or could vary, and parallel to whether the causal explanation of the dream phenomenon corresponds to Psychology or Physiology, has been present since an ancient theory was first proposed. Who considers dreams as a disturbance of rest: "we would not have dreamed if our rest had not been disturbed by a specific cause, the dream being, therefore, a reaction to such a disturbance? Regarding the sources of sleep, Freud recognizes the existence of four different types of dream sources, a differentiation that has also served as a basis for classifying dreams: external (objective) sensory stimuli, such as an intense light that reaches our eyes, a noise to our ears or a smell to our nose; the internal (subjective) sensory stimuli, in reference to those subjective, visual or auditory sensations, that hardly cross the threshold of perception and that in the waking state are known to us as luminous chaos of the dark visual field, ringing of ears, etc.; internal (organic) somatic stimuli, the result of the excitement or alteration of our internal organs, which in health state hardly give us any news of their existence, but which during states of excitement or illness become a source of sensations, mostly painful, equivalent to stimuli from outside; and, finally, the purely psychic sources of stimulation, a not insignificant oneiric source that supposes that the interests of the awakened life (occupations and daily worries) pass to the state of rest, justifying the presence of some of the contents of the dream.

4. Oneiric theories. Since sleep has become an important object of study for different disciplines (biology, physiology, psychology, etc.), a more than a considerable number of dream theories have emerged that try to reveal its enigmatic nature and its controversial function. Even though they are not the most rigorous and successful, among them Freud highlights:

a) Those theories that consider that during sleep, the psychic activity of wakefulness lasts. According to them, the soul does not sleep. Its processes remain intact but subject to the conditions of the state of rest, different from those of wakefulness, it produces, even when operating normally, different yields: dreams. Unfortunately, these theories do not explain why we dream or why the complicated mechanism of the psychic apparatus continues to function even after being placed in circumstances for which it is not prepared. The only appropriate reactions in this situation would be to sleep without dreams or to wake up when a disturbing stimulus occurs, but never to dream.

b) Those theories that accept that sleep is the result of a decrease in psychic activity and a weakening of coherence, theories, widely applauded by medical authors and, in general, by the scientific world, from which it follows that rest extends to the soul but fails to isolate it from the outside world completely, but penetrates its mechanism, making it temporarily unusable. Thus, the dream phenomenon must be considered as the result of an imperfect performance of the soul as a partial vigil, which allows us to explain the absurdity of some of its contents. Regarding the validity of this theory of partial wakefulness, numerous objections have been raised, most of them emphasizing its inability to explain: "Firstly, rest and wakefulness, and secondly, why some forces of the soul act in the dream while others rest" (Burdach, 1830).

c) In a third section, we can group those theories that ascribe to the dreaming soul the power to perform certain psychic functions that in the waking situation it cannot carry out or can only do very incompletely. The state of rest is, then, the time-lapse in which the soul recovers and accumulates new energies for daytime labor. To put it another way, dreams protect us against the monotony and vulgarity of existence, and they are a kind of psychic vacation. Therefore, we will have to see in them "a charming faculty and a friendly company in our pilgrimage towards the tomb."

5. Sleep function. Based on his extensive studies on dreams, Freud thought that dreaming fulfills two basic functions in psychic life: a) protecting the rest of the dreamer by converting the material and stimuli that could potentially disturb his rest into images and content type of dreaming; and b) satisfying during rest, even if virtually, those desires that the dreamer has not been able to satisfy in the waking state. To put it in other words, far from being foolish or absurd, dreams for Freud are the guardian of sleep, while representing a curious and very particular way of satisfying desires. Freud's theory seems supported by the fact that the small alterations that occur during rest are often incorporated in dreams, preventing them from waking us up at night. An intense nose, a change in temperature, hunger pangs, or strong pressure on the bladder can be incorporated into dream material (directly or symbolically), preventing the dreamer from finally waking up. Freud also proposes a second and more important function of dreaming: his famous theory of wish-fulfillment. Unmet needs, frustrated yearnings, contrary desires, are fully compensated during sleep, thanks to mysterious alchemy, in all its details, although, virtually, it is true. So much so that even the role of the guardian of sleep can be considered as a wish-fulfillment, since, after all, we dream because we want to stay asleep.

6. Structure of the dream. Thanks to the work of dream interpretation, Freud concludes that in the structure of dreams it is necessary to differentiate between the manifest content and the latent content — latent ideas — while proposing a new line of research for psychoanalysis: analyzing the relations between both contents and find out by which process the manifest content has emerged from the latest ideas. As for the manifest content, we must say what the dream develops before us, what we remember, and what we submit to interpretation. It is the dream as it is presented by the subject that carries out the narration, the difficult work of the dreamlike elaboration that, arbitrarily, presents it to us as if it were a hieroglyph, for whose solution we will have to translate each of its signs into the language of the latent ideas. Regarding the latent content, we will say that it is the experience (desires, experiences, memories, etc.) that motivates the dream and gives rise to the manifest content. It consists of daily remains, body impressions, childhood memories, and transference residues that give meaning to the manifest content. It constitutes the set of meanings to which the analysis leads and is, of course, before the manifest content and cause.

This being the case, we must now ask why it is necessary to make this distinction between latent content and manifest content, what are the reasons that justify such differentiation and, of course, why the contents of the dream are not identical. Freud, apparently, is very clear about the answer to these three questions: censorship, it is responsible for the deformation of the dream and, therefore, for the latent/manifest differentiation to which we have referred. Oneiric censorship is defined by Freud as that function that tends to prevent latent ideas from accessing consciousness, that is, the function that stops the transformation of latent ideas into manifest content, a function that acts by suppressing or merging elements of the dream, changing its hierarchy, substituting one element for another — or a symbol — displacing its center of gravity and/or its importance, etc. A task that he carries out against those deplorable ideas that we don't even want to think about.

7. The dream production. Freud describes dream-making as the work of the dreamer's psyche to transform latent dream ideas into manifest content. From this perspective, the dream that we awakened to remember would only be a summary of the dream-making process that, based on latent ideas, the dreamer has carried out while sleeping. As the subject cannot explicitly dream of everything he really wants, envies or ambitions without being assailed by an insufferable feeling of guilt (repression), in a Machiavellian display of adaptation, he masks those latent ideas that are rejectable from an ethical point of view, aesthetic, social or cultural so that they can find through the dream a way of expression and satisfaction, even if it is only virtual. We must say, therefore, that the dream-making work is completed with the presentation of a story (dream) that runs during the rest, a story that has been built from the latest ideas, which are those that reveal the true sense of sleep.

To carry out this arduous masking task, the dream-making basically uses five mechanisms: condensation, displacement, symbolization, dramatization, and the transformation of ideas into visual images.

a) Condensation. Condensation is considered by Freud as one of the most important mechanisms in the dream-making work. Specifically, he defines it as that oneiric elaboration mechanism by which various ideas or elements of the latent content come together in a single image or representation of the manifest content, a grouping that, in his opinion, is mainly due to economic causes. In fact, Freud considers that the manifest content is nothing more than the abbreviated translation of a group of latent ideas that have been grouped into a disharmonic unit in the manifest content (for example, a character made up of fragments or parts of others).

The manifesto is concise, poor, and laconic compared to the breadth and richness of latent ideas. In short, the condensation process makes the account of the manifest content much shorter than the description of the latent content.

b) Displacement. Displacement is an unconscious psychic process theorized by Freud in the framework of the analysis of dreams. Basically, it is an oneiric elaboration mechanism that, using an associative slip, transforms the essential elements of a latent content into secondary details of a manifest content. Although it can also act in other ways (for example, causing one element to be replaced by another), it is a mechanism that generally intervenes in the elaboration of dreams, causing the accent, interest, intensity and/or significance of a latent element is detached from it to go on to impregnate elements of the manifest content originally little or little intense, although linked by an associative chain to the first. In this way, the fundamental meaning of the dream can appear in the manifest content as an accessory or secondary element, and, conversely, the most important element of the manifest content can be presented as a secondary element of authentic meaning. Thus, the displacement causes the meaning to be transferred from the central part of the dream to its accessory places, thus hiding from the dreamer the true nature of his dreams.

c) Symbolization. It is, without a doubt, the most important dream elaboration mechanism. It consists of the indirect and figurative representation through symbols of a latent idea of a conflict or of an unconscious desire. This makes the analyst's task of understanding the dream essentially an interpretation task: the analyst has to move from the level of the symbol — located at the level of manifest content — to the level of meaning — located at the level of latent content. Religion, myths and fables, and art are also modes of symbolization that can be interpreted in the same terms as dreams. For Freud, the knowledge of symbols is not conscious, but neither is it arbitrary. Most of them are universal and require an interpretation of erotic or sexual nature, but must always be interpreted, taking into account the biography and personality of the subject.

d) Dramatization. Thanks to this oneiric elaboration mechanism, the dream presents, albeit covertly, distorted or surreptitiously, a latent idea, a conflict or a desire of the subject in a more or less complete story format; the dream turns a static reality, such as appetite, a need or past experience, into a dynamic reality in which various characters intervene and interact and develop an authentic drama.

e) Transformation of ideas into visual images. There is no doubt that the tasks of condensation, displacement, and symbolization are fundamental when it comes to an understanding and explaining the process of making dreams. However, we will still have to add another way, less intense but equally valid, of dreamlike deformation: the transformation of ideas into images. If, as it seems, we dream in the form of sensory images, there must be a psychic process that is responsible for transforming the latent ideas of the dream into images of this type. The argument is quite simple; if the manifest content of the dream is almost always made up of visual situations, the latent ideas must, above all, have to adopt a disposition that makes them suitable for this peculiar form of exposition.

8. Secondary elaboration. This action supposes a second time in the work of elaboration of the dream, affecting, consequently, the products already elaborated by the other oneiric elaboration mechanisms (condensation, displacement, symbolization, etc.). Ultimately, it is a dreamlike elaboration mechanism that aspires to give coherence to the dream through the selection and arrangement of the material, the insertion of associative links, and inclusion in an intelligible context. The most perceptible consequence of this action is that the dream loses its primitive aspect of delirium and approaches the context of a rational event. Subtracting the dream from its primitive appearance of absurdity and incoherence, filling its gaps, making a partial or total recomposition of its elements and recomposing it in such a way that it can be presented in the form of a relatively coherent and understandable script, is the aim of what Freud called secondary elaboration or also the consideration of representability.

Psychopathology Of Everyday Life

Psychopathology of everyday life (1901) is a work in which Freud, based on a subject as trivial as forgetfulness, errors, and mistakes, tries to delve into the unconscious mechanisms of the human psyche. In it, the creator of psychoanalysis expresses with great simplicity and no less insight the existence of a double functioning in psychic life: the conscious and the unconscious, a double functioning that, at times, ends up causing a real short circuit in saying and/or in the doing of the subject (forgetfulness, absent-mindedness, clumsiness, loss, etc.). In fact, the study detailed of phenomena of such anodyne appearance allow Freud to argue in an easily understandable way the endemic influence of unconscious material on the whole of conscious life. So much so that Peter Gay, in his biography of Freud (1988), goes so far as to affirm that the father of psychoanalysis deliberately chose the interpretation of these small facts of daily life as the starting point of his fruitful work.

Freud, apparently, was very clear that the goal of this work was to attract attention to things that everyone knows and experiences, to current everyday events, to subject them to rigorous scientific examination and to demonstrate, without any doubt, the accuracy of his proposals on the unconscious psyche. Furthermore, a tenacious defender of the thesis of an absolute psychic determinism that postulates that every physical event, including human thought and actions, is causally determined by the unshakable cause-consequence chain, Freud tries to

147

demonstrate, as he recalls several times in the book, that the field of action of psychoanalysis should not be limited to the domain of pathology. On the contrary, to the wisdom acquired thanks to the conscientious analysis of the different clinical cases, we must add the wisdom derived from the experiences of everyday life, which, according to Freud, should never be denied a place in acquisitions, of the science.

Specifically, Psychopathology of everyday life is a work that is divided into twelve chapters dedicated to the different forms of forgetfulness, lapses, errors, awkwardness and other failed acts, a sensible division whose criteria is as arbitrary as descriptive, since as the author himself acknowledges, the phenomena studied have a logical internal coherence to which every book testifies. The first chapter, for example, deals with the forgetting of proper names, a period of memory that Freud tries to explain, arguing that human beings always try to forget what bothers, displeases or disturbs us, and which therefore has a lot to do with the repression mechanism. The summary of the conditions for forgetting names is as follows: a) that there be a certain provision for forgetting the name in question; b) that a repressive process took place a short time before; c) an associative link is created between the name that is not remembered and the previously repressed element.

In the next two chapters, Freud uses several examples of forgetting names, foreign words and series of words in which he believes that this proposal is confirmed, a proposal that extends to all failed acts: the forgotten or deformed comes into connection, for any associative path, with an unconscious psychic content, from which that influence manifests itself in the form of forgetfulness, mistakes, errors and/or lapses. It should not be forgotten, he assures us, that the analysis of forgetting leads us, almost always, to intimate matters of the analyzed, sometimes even unpleasant and painful for him.

Failed act:

An act in which the explicitly pursued result is not obtained but manifests a different form of expression and still contrary to the original intention of the subject. It assumes the existence of two purposes: the disturbed and the disturbing. It can be in action, in verbal speech, or in gesture.

Features:

1. The subject is capable of performing the act correctly.

2. It is a momentary and temporary disturbance.

3. It is within the limits of normality.

4. The incorrectness of the act is immediately recognized.

5. It does not affect important areas of behavior.

6. There is an association between what is repressed and what is not remembered.

Childhood memories and cloaking memories are addressed, memories in which, apparently, the subject seems to have kept the most insignificant and secondary of his life, while the really important events do not seem to have left any mark in his memory. These indifferent childhood memories, Freud observes, owe their existence to a process of displacement, being nothing more than a substitute representation of other truly important impressions, the memory of which can be extracted from them through psychic analysis, but whose direct reproduction is hindered by a resistance (hence the expression "cover-up memory ").

As for the temporal relationship between this concealing memory and the transcendental fact that is hidden behind it, Freud believes it is necessary to differentiate three types of displacement: regressive, progressive, and simultaneous. Displacement is called regressive when the content of the covering memory belongs to the first years of childhood, and the life experiences replaced by it in memory — which remain unconscious — correspond to later years of the subject's life. On the contrary, in those cases in which an indifferent impression of early childhood is fixed in memory as a covering memory because of its association with previous experience, against whose reproduction a resistance rises (what is chronologically important is behind the covering memory), the displacement is called progressive.

Finally, the third type of displacement can be presented, the simultaneous one, in which the covering memory is associated with the impression that it conceals not only for its content but also for its continuity in time.

Freud analyzes oral mistakes (lapsus linguae), mistakes in reading and writing, forgetfulness of impressions and purposes, errors and misguided acts combined, giving them the same treatment as forgetfulness, since which considers that, like memory lapses, they are daily episodes that are accepted naturally without suspecting that they contain a covert-unconscious-intention, which cannot be brought to consciousness except through penetrating analysis. Now, to be included in the order of phenomena to which this explanation can be applied, a failed psychic functioning must meet the following requirements:

a) Not exceed to a certain extent what common sense considers as "Within the limits of normal."

b) Possess the character of momentary and temporary disturbance. The subject immediately recognizes the incorrectness of the act since he has been able to execute it correctly previously.

c) Be explained as a "lack of attention" or a "coincidence," since there is not the slightest hint of intent in carrying out the act.

Thus, and convinced that the failed acts "express something that the actor himself does not suspect," something that "escapes conscious intention," Freud tries to explain the presence of such acts in our daily life by enunciating the following principle: "Certain insufficiencies of our psychic functioning and certain apparently unintended acts are shown to be motivated and determined by unknown motives of conscience when subjected to the psychoanalytic investigation." In this way, the cases of forgetfulness, the mistakes made in the exposition of subjects that are perfectly known to us, the mistakes in reading and writing, the acts of erroneous term and the so-called accidental acts, all phenomena in which the main is the loss of intention, they become material for analysis, being able to refer to "an incompletely repressed psychic material, which is rejected by the conscience, but which has not been stripped of all capacity to externalize itself."

Finally, we will have to comment that Psychopathology of everyday life concludes with an exemplified chapter dedicated to the questions of determinism, beliefs and superstition, three original and controversial topics whose development forces Freud to confess that, unfortunately, "I belong to those Unworthy individuals in whose eyes the spirits hide their activity and from whom the supernatural departs so that nothing has ever happened to me that has brought about in me the faith in the wonderful. Like all men, I have had presentiments and misfortunes that have happened to me, but these have never corresponded to those. My presentiments have not been realized, and the misfortunes have come to me unannounced ... Nor have any of the presentiments that have been reported to me by my patients ever been able to achieve my recognition as a real phenomenon". It would be, therefore, correct to affirm that the failed act is, in synthesis, a kind of betrayal that our psyche does to us by revealing an unconscious desire or intention, a betrayal that finds its reason for being in the evidence that "in the psychic, there is nothing arbitrary or indeterminate."

Psychoanalytical Theory Of Neurosis

As is known, the theory and technique of psychoanalysis

base their fundamental premises on clinical data from the study of neuroses. Understood as "psychogenic conditions whose symptoms are the symbolic expression of a psychic conflict that has its roots in the subject's childhood history and constitutes commitments between desire and defense" (Laplanche and Pontalis, 1987), neuroses still provide the original material more solid and reliable for the formulation of psychoanalytic theory. So much so that to understand the theory of psychoanalytic technique, Greenson assures in his Technique and Practice of Psychoanalysis (1976), it is necessary to have a broad practical knowledge of the psychoanalytic theory of neuroses.

Historical background

The Scottish physician first used the term neurosis and chemist William Cullen (1710-1790) in his Synopsis nosologiae exact (1769) to refer to sensory and motor disorders caused by diseases of the nervous system. In this ancient work, Cullen describes neuroses as "preternatural affections of sense and movement in which pyrexia — non-symptomatic fever — is in no way part of the primitive disease, and which does not depend on a local condition of the organs, but of a more general affection of the nervous system and of the powers that regulate the sense and the movement," a description that presents the neuroses as authentic physiological and general nervous ailments without fever or injury.

After Cullen's Synopsis nosologiae methodical burst onto the clinical stage, the definition of this "sense and movement " disorder confronts representatives of medicine. On the one hand, the defenders of the pathological approach to neurosis, with Philippe Pinel (1745-1826) at the head — which considers mental illnesses as a disorder of the cerebral faculties; on the other, the supporters of a more functionalist approach to neurosis, with Juan Martin Charcot (1825-1893) at the forefront — which maintains the existence of a supposed dynamic injury in neurotic manifestations. Somehow, however, both positions coincide in the supposed biological basis of the neuroses.

Meanwhile, various diseases are breaking away from the common trunk of neuroses when their strictly organic origin is discovered. We refer specifically to progressive general paralysis, dementia, catalepsy, tetanus, asthma, epilepsy, and neuralgia, a select and varied group of diseases that, according to a questioned differential diagnosis of exclusion, ended up falling in the domains of neurosis. Thus, the truth is that by the end of the 19th century, the body of neuroses had been reduced to psychasthenia or obsessive neurosis, hysteria, hypochondria, and neurasthenia, a few but very active ailments that brought neurologists upside down of the time. Among them, we will highlight Pierre Janet (1859-1947), a French psychologist and neurologist who, in addition to founding the *Journal de Psychologie normal et pathologique* (1904), made important contributions to the modern study of mental and emotional disorders. Specifically, Janet considers that neurosis is a mental disorder caused by a decrease in psychological tension, a decrease in tension due to chronic brain exhaustion that alters the subject's psychic reality.

Nevertheless, Freud (1856-1939) deserves credit for incorporating one of the most ingenious and revolutionary approaches in the argument on the subject of neuroses: the notion of psychic conflict. Indeed, already in the Studies on Hysteria (1895), Freud discovers to us how, as he approaches the pathogenic memories in the course of the cure, he finds an increasingly energetic resistance in the subject; a resistance that is nothing more than the current expression of an internal defense that stands up against the conflicting desires, the contradictory feelings and the incompatible representations that the analysis tries to reveal. Likewise, we must not forget that Freud, since 1893, has opted for a much more psychological — and, therefore, much less biological — interpretation of neuroses, especially hysteria, phobias and obsessive neuroses (psychoneurosis), having discovered that the cause of such conditions is in psychosexual traumas produced in early times of life.

Etiology of neurosis

As a result of diligent clinical work, Freud was able to develop a complex — and, at the same time, changing — theory about neuroses and mental illness. In his opinion, neuroses should originate from unconscious instinctual and emotional motivations, which would be tremendously active and would manifest themselves symbolically in the form of organic (paralysis, anesthesia, seizures, etc.) and psychological symptoms (anguish, fear, depression, melancholy, etc.), symptoms that, on the other hand, characterize the classic clinical pictures of the so-called "nervous diseases." But, let's go by parts. In 1889, Freud considered that hysteria, synonymous with neurosis at that time, was the result of the subject's fixation on an intensely emotional nonspecific experience. This experience played a primary role in the genesis of the disease and the father of psychoanalysis he referred to using the word trauma. Thus, any event in the life of the subject that exceeded his capacity for control and psychic elaboration of emotional excitement had to be considered traumatic. Therefore, it had to be interpreted as the immediate cause of neurosis (trauma theory).

On the other hand, Freud is convinced that there is a certain constitutional background in neuroses in which hereditary factors play a fundamental role, which undoubtedly points to a certain congenital predisposition towards such ailments. However, and despite this firm conviction, clinical experience shows him, case after case, that the etiology of neurosis is due, preferably, to intense emotional experiences related to the individual's biographical process, especially with his childhood. In fact, in his Fragmentary Analysis of a Hysteria (1901), Freud assures us that if we do not want to be forced to abandon traumatic theory definitively "we will have to go back to the childhood of the subject to look for influences and impressions that may have acted analogous to that of trauma, a setback all the more necessary since even in the investigation of cases whose first symptoms had not arisen in childhood, I have always found something that has prompted me to pursue the history of patients until that early period."

In any case, from 1900 Freud was forced to limit the scope of the trauma concept, affirming — and this had much to do with his patient Dora — that it was not an unspecific emotional experience that caused the neuroses, but that his nature was eminently sexual. From this moment on, and according to what he called seduction theory, he maintained that hysteria was produced by an early sexual experience, which occurred between the ages of four and five, in which the initiative corresponded to another person (generally an adult), an experience that could range from simple insinuations in the form of words or gestures, to a more or less defined sexual assault, that the subject suffered passively with fright (a state that occurs when you enter a dangerous situation without being prepared; the accent falls on the surprise factor). This early traumatic experience left an indelible mark on the subject's psyche, appearing later in the disease represented by the symptoms.

Constitutional factor Trauma

Now, as Freud went deeper into the study of clinical cases treated according to the technical principles of psychoanalysis, he was able to verify that, although most of the patients reported traumatic events of a sexual nature that occurred in their childhood, the investigations carried out among the relatives and friends of the patient showed that these events could never have occurred, and that, therefore, they should be considered as products of the subject's fantasy. Freud himself, in a letter sent to his friend

Fliess on September 21, 1897, believes it necessary to reveal the great secret that has been slowly revealed to him in recent months: "I no longer believe in my neurotic," the seduction scenes that he relates are, at times, the fruit of his fantasy.

As a result of this discovery, Freud restricts the value of seduction in the genesis of neuroses, assigning, instead, greater etiological importance to fantasies, which he considers a nuclear factor in the appearance and persistence of such pathologies (theory of fantasies). The reasons for this drastic change, moreover, seem clear:

a) Not all neurotics have suffered early sexual trauma.

b) Not all people who have suffered real trauma have subsequently developed a neurosis.

c) Traumatic experiences, while still being sexual, could very well not be genital, since, for psychoanalysis, sexual is everything that allows the rapid release of tension (everything genital is sexual, but not everything sexual is genital).

For these reasons, Freud is forced to acknowledge his errors: "My analytical research first fell into the error of overestimating sexual seduction or initiation as the source of infantile sexual manifestations and the germ of the production of neurotic symptoms. Overcoming this error was achieved by discovering the extraordinary role that fantasy played in the psychic life of neurotics, frankly more decisive for neurosis than external reality " in fact, and although until the end of his life Freud did not stop insisting on the existence and pathogenic value of the seduction scenes lived by the subject in childhood, from 1897 the etiological scope of the trauma diminished in favor of fantasies and fixations to the various libidinal phases.

It can be said, then, that the traumatic point of view, even when Freud does not abandon it, is integrated into a much broader conception of neurosis, a conception that involves other factors, such as the sexual constitution and child history. Furthermore, it is strikingly noteworthy that, in this scheme elaborated by Freud in the Introductory Lessons to Psychoanalysis (1917), the term traumatic is not used to refer to the childhood experiences that are at the origin of fixations, but that it is used to designate an event that comes to the subject in the second stage of their biographical history. Therefore, the importance and scope of the trauma are restricted and subordinated to the later history of the subject (accidental events of the adult), coming to be assimilated in this proposal to what Freud, in previous formulations, considered simply frustration.

In any case, the arguments collected by Freud in The New Introductory Lessons to Psychoanalysis (1932) and Inhibition, Symptoms, and Anguish (1925), allow us to complete this etiological equation of neurosis by adding the dynamic perspective. This perspective is facilitated by the fixation, regression, and sublimation concepts:

- Hereditary factor
- Fetal experiences
- Maternal experiences
- Children's experiences
- Predisposition

- Trigger event
- Reactivation
- Oral fixation

In this explanatory scheme, hereditary factors (together with maternal experiences — which would act on the fetus and fetal experiences that would act on the mother) represent what in psychoanalysis has been called the constitutional factor of neurosis, a factor that, as we have previously pointed out, points to a certain congenital predisposition of the individual towards such diseases.

However, we cannot forget that childhood experiences, especially if they have been emotionally intense, play a fundamental role in the etiology of neuroses first, because they leave an indelible mark on the life of every human being. Second, because they determine the fixation points linked to childhood to which the regression mechanism — a psychodynamic process that involves the return to archaic evolutionary stages of the libidinal organization — drags the subject when, after having faced a traumatic event that has occurred and having unsuccessful in the attempt, frustration and disillusionment arise.

Freud himself, in lesson XXIII of his Introductory Lessons to Psychoanalysis (1917), does not hesitate to affirm that it is a mistake to "undermine the importance of the events that occurred during the subject's childhood and to emphasize, instead, that of those corresponding to the life of their ancestors or their maturity," an error that could be avoided if child events were given " a very special meaning since by taking place at a time when the development of the subject is still unfinished, they bring more serious consequences and are susceptible to traumatic action."

In this sense, and returning to the scheme that concerns us, it is worth remembering that when an unexpected traumatic event generates frustration and, due to this, the libido — psychic energy of the sexual drives that your regime finds in terms of desire and aspirations amorous — stops flowing freely and stagnates, the events of infantile sexual life act as true centers of attraction for the immobilized libido, to which it returns every time that its satisfaction, in reality, is impeded.

When libido cannot flow freely, it is inhibited and stagnant in the first place. If also, it finds difficulties redirecting the tension that the traumatic event (sublimation) entails, it returns to earlier positions and tries to discharge again to that level. If also at that level the satisfaction of the libido is impeded, and the sublimation is still insufficient to mitigate the tension generated by the traumatic event that occurred, the anxiety is triggered, the anguish that the subject perceives as an alarm signal, proceeding to activate their defense mechanisms. If the defense mechanisms that the subject activates are sufficient, timely, and successful, the anxiety is reduced or neutralized; if, on the contrary, they are insufficient, inconvenient, or objectionable, the anguish remains, increases and becomes a symptom.

Defense mechanisms

In his 1894 essay Defense Neuropsychosis, Freud introduces the concept of defense and places it at the origin of hysterical phenomena, since, after analyzing several cases of acquired hysteria, various phobias and obsessive representations, and certain hallucinatory psychoses, he concludes that an experience, representation or sensation, when it is intolerable for the subject, can generate an affection so painful that, if it is not elaborated mentally and is excluded from consciousness, can give rise to various pathological manifestations. Well, the different mental operations that the subject uses to free himself from these intolerable representations, which almost always settle in the field of experience or sexual sensitivity, is what begins to be considered "defenses" in these first moments of psychoanalysis.

Until the appearance of The Interpretation of Dreams (1900), the term "defense" continues to appear in Freud's work as an indisputable reference to the set of operations with which the ego (region of the personality in charge of protecting us from all disturbance) defends against intolerable representations. However, it must also be said that, from 1900, Freud preferred to use the term "repression" to refer to the defensive process aimed at subjugating the intolerable experience: "repression" as I have begun to say instead of defense.

In any case, from this arbitrary Freudian preference, it should not be inferred that repression equals defense, on the contrary, the mechanism of repression constitutes for the psychoanalytic plot the paradigm of defensive operations, while the defense is a generic concept that designates a general tendency to the reduction or suppression of all excitement likely to endanger the integrity of the individual.

Subsequently, in Inhibition, Symptom, and Anguish (1926), Freud returns to the investigation of defense mechanisms, striving to clarify the convoluted question of its equivalence with the term "repression," a question he intends to conclude with what he calls the "restoration of the old concept of defense," that is, invoking the need for a global concept that includes, in addition to repression, other defense methods such as displacement, isolation, conversion or sublimation. Let us not forget that Freud himself, when he had already included repression among the defense mechanisms when commenting on Endless and endless analysis (1937) the book by his daughter Anna, The Self and Defense Mechanisms (1936), writes:

"It was from one of these mechanisms, that of repression, that the study of neurotic processes had its beginning. He never doubted that it was not the only procedure that the self could use for its purposes. But repression is something very peculiar and is now more clearly differentiated from the other mechanisms than these among them."

Defense neuro psychosis (1894)

It can be said, then, that defense mechanisms are the "different types of operations in which defense can be specified" (Laplanche and Pontalis, 1987), or, if you prefer, those unconscious psychodynamic processes through which the subject it tries to harmoniously integrate the demands of its internal world with the demands of the external world. Namely:

Repression- It is the operation which the subject tries to reject or maintain in the unconscious representations (thoughts, images, memories, etc.) linked to a drive to be considered unpleasant, threatening, or destructive from the ethical point of view, aesthetic, social or cultural. Repression is particularly manifest in hysteria, although it also plays an important role in other mental disorders and normal psychology. It can be considered a universal psychic process since it is at the origin of the unconscious constitution as an autonomous domain separated from the rest of the psyche. Let's say of it:

a) What is the earliest-onset defense mechanism?

b) That tries to prevent the direct satisfaction of the drive.

c) That at some point, the repressed has had to be conscious.

Regression - The unconscious psychodynamic process involves the return to forms of behavior and satisfaction typical of previous stages of development that were believed to have been overcome. In a formal sense, regression designates the transition to modes of expression and behavior at a lower level, from complexity, structuring, and differentiation. It is a kind of return, back in the evolutionary process, towards more satisfactory forms of behavior and relationship in the face of the frustrating nature of current living conditions. In any case, if we listen to Freud in the passage added in 1914 to The Interpretation of Dreams, we will have to distinguish three kinds of regressions:

a) Topical, in the sense of the scheme of the psychic apparatus (cons - icons).

b) Temporary, since the oldest psychic formations are reactivated.

c) Formal, since it goes from the usual modes of expression and representation to more primitive ones.

Isolation - Defense mechanism, typical above all in obsessive neurosis, which consists in isolating a thought or behavior so that its connections with other thoughts or with the rest of the subject's existence are broken. Among the isolation processes, we can mention pauses in the course of thought, ritual formulas, and, in general, all the measures that allow us to establish a hiatus in the temporal succession of thoughts or acts.

Reactive training - Attitude or psychological habit of opposite sense to a repressed desire and that has been constituted as a reaction against it (for example, the modesty that opposes exhibitionist tendencies). It is a defense mechanism that involves reinforcing the dam of repression to such an extent that the subject carries out the opposite behavior that made him drive his drive.

Projection - Operation through which the subject expels from himself and locates in the other (person or thing) qualities, feelings, and desires that moral censure repudiates in oneself. It is a defense of very archaic origin that is seen to act particularly in paranoia, but also in some normal forms of thought, such as superstition. It supposes, in any case, the failure of the repression.

Introjection - Unconscious psychological process evidenced by psychoanalytic research through which the subject makes fantasized pass, from "outside" to "inside", characteristics, qualities or traits of other people or objects, this way, they become their characteristics.

Fantasy - An imaginary scenario in which the subject is present and represents, in more or less distorted by defensive processes, the realization of a desire that otherwise could not be satisfied. It can be presented under different appearances: conscious fantasies — daydreams, unconscious fantasies —subliminal dream — and original fantasies — linked to unconscious desire. Frequent in adolescence, fantasy can become pathological if used by adults with great frustrations.

Sublimation - The unconscious psychological process postulated by Freud explains certain human activities that have no relation to sexuality, but that would find their energy in the force of the sexual drive. In general, sublimation is spoken of as a process by which the subject derives part – or all – of the energy from the sexual drive towards the achievement of socially recognized purposes. It has ideal values and does not involve pathology at all.

Rationalization - The procedure by which the subject tries to give a coherent explanation, from the logical point of view, or acceptable from the moral point of view to an attitude, an act, an idea, a feeling, etc., whose true motives do not perceive. It involves the search for logical and ethical reasons that justify an action that is motivated by unconscious factors.

Conversion - Defense mechanism thanks to which the subject transforms the repudiated desire into a bodily manifestation. It consists of the transposition of psychic conflict and an attempt to resolve it in somatic symptoms (phonation disorders, allergies, dizziness), motor (paralysis) or sensitive (anesthesia or localized pain).

Denial - The unconscious psychological process, by which the subject, despite formulating one of his previously repressed wishes, thoughts, or feelings, continues to defend himself by denying that it belongs to him. Annoying representation is excluded by rejecting the perception linked to that representation. Reality itself is denied; it is as if the event had not taken place.

Punishment - The defense mechanism by which the subject tends to carry out certain behaviors tending to compensate the feelings of guilt originated by the existence of certain behaviors, desires, and feelings that the moral conscience repudiates.

Cancellation - Psychological mechanism by which the subject performs an act or carries out a certain activity to cancel the meaning of another previously carried out.

Displacement - A defense mechanism that consists of separating the affective charge from the painful representation, passing it to catheterize (load with psychic energy) other more or less related mental content symbolically with annoying representation. The accent, interest, and intensity of the representation come off to impregnate other representations that were originally not very intense, although linked to the first by an associative chain.

Neurosis classification

According to Enrique Freijo (1987), the term neurosis has two meanings in psychoanalysis that must be differentiated, the descriptive and the etiological. From the descriptive point of view, the word "neurosis" refers to a certain group of disorders that are characterized by peculiar conjunction of signs and symptoms, both psychic and somatic.

From the etiological point of view, it is a word that tells us of the existence of a psychic conflict of an unconscious nature, of a private conflict between one or more impulses that tend to discharge them and the psychic forces within the subject that oppose to the person, in short, of a hidden conflict that, to a greater or lesser extent, is symbolically expressed through different combinations of signs and symptoms.

It can be said, then, that neurotic reaction is a pathology of interpersonal relationships. This pathology manifests itself in somatic dysfunctions, psychic disorders and behavioral disturbances, a pathology whose main cause is the existence of a psychic conflict which, given its unconscious nature, causes symptoms to be experienced subjectively as inexplicable and irrational.

In summary, psychoanalysis has come to demonstrate that

neurosis is the result of the subject's inability to adequately resolve the unconscious conflicts that exist in the psyche, conflicts that have their roots in childhood history, and are expressed symbolically in the form of symptoms.

By this, we mean that no matter where you look, neurotic conflict is nothing but the dramatic consequence of the failure of the ego in trying to carry out its work of synthesis and integration on the three different fronts on which it must be carried out: that of instinctual impulses, that of moral demands and that of external reality. This unfortunate failure gives priority to neurotic symptoms.

Adapted from E. Freijo (1987)

Current Neuroses - This group of neuroses' origin should not be sought in childhood conflicts but present experiences, normally related to disorders in sexual life. The symptoms do not constitute a symbolic and overdetermined expression, but rather result directly from the lack or inadequacy of sexual satisfaction.

Neurasthenia - Condition described by the American doctor George Beard (1839-1883), whose clinical picture revolves around physical fatigue of nervous origin. It includes symptoms from the most diverse registers: headaches, spinal paresthesias, vague pain, boredom, lack of interest, and impoverishment of sexual activity. Its origin points to an inadequate satisfaction of the sexual drive in adults, specifically masturbation.

The neurosis of Anxiety - Psychogenic condition in which anguish (anxious expectation, attacks of anguish, or somatic equivalents of it) appears as the main symptom. It is specifically characterized by the accumulation of sexual arousal, the arousal that is directly transformed into a symptom without psychic mediation. It is associated with situations of forced abstinence, sexual overexertion, and continued practice of coitus interruptus, situations, and experiences, all of which lead to strong frustration in sexual satisfaction. There is no harmony between the physical and the psychological response in terms of satisfaction: there can be sexual intercourse, and yet there can be no satisfaction.

Psychoneurosis - In contrast to current neuroses, this is the name given to the group of psychogenic disorders whose symptoms constitute the symbolic expression of childhood conflicts. Also called transference neuroses, they differ from narcissistic neuroses in that the libido is generally displaced on objects rather than on the self. They are the only ones capable of psychoanalytic treatment.

Hysterical Neurosis - Psychic affection of very varied clinical pictures whose two best isolated symptomatic forms are conversion hysteria, in which the psychic conflict is symbolized in the most diverse bodily symptoms (cyanosis, urticarias, hemorrhages, lethargy, etc.), paroxysmal (attacks of hiccups, tremors, tics, an emotional crisis with theatricality, etc.) or long-lasting (anesthesia, paralysis, pharyngeal <bolo> feeling, etc.), and the hysteria of anguish, in which the anguish is fixed more or less stable to a certain external object (phobias). The regression of libido is a pathology linked to the phallic phase of libidinal evolution since it correlates with the Castration complex and imposes the approach and resolution of the Oedipus Complex.

Obsessive-compulsive neurosis - A form of neurosis isolated by Freud in the years 1894-1895 that constitutes one of the great pictures of the psychoanalytic clinic. In its most typical form, the latent psychic conflict is expressed by the so-called compulsive symptoms:

a) Parasitic ideas of an obsessive nature, which are recognized as their own despite accepting their absurdity.

b) Compulsion to perform undesirable acts.

c) Constant struggle to escape these thoughts and tendencies.

d) Performance of certain ceremonies tending to conjure obsessive ideas.

e) A type of thought characterized by doubts, misgivings, and scruples; symptoms that inevitably lead to inhibitions of thought and action. The regression of libido is a pathology linked to the sadistic-anal phase (secondary anal) of libidinal evolution, a phase in which the triad order, greed, and stubbornness appear to us as a paradigm of anal eroticism.

Narcissistic Neuroses - In contrast to the transference neuroses (psychoneurosis), Freud thus names the group of mental illnesses characterized by the withdrawal of libido from the ego. It is a term that currently tends to disappear from psychiatric and psychoanalytic language, but which is found in Freud's writings as an expression equivalent to "psychosis", conditions to which Freud, at least in the early days of psychoanalysis, prefers to call "paraphrenias" — a term proposed by Kraepelin to designate chronic delusional psychoses that, like paranoia, are not accompanied by intellectual weakness or evolve into dementia, but resemble schizophrenia in their delusional constructions based on hallucinations and fables.

Manic-depressive psychosis - A term coined by Kraepelin to refer to recurrent manic and depressive disorders that, having common features — both are affective disorders — followed one another (cyclical evolution) and had a very similar prognosis and evolution (periodic episodes). In the manic phase — a state of exhilaration and excitement disproportionate to the circumstances the subject is experiencing — the most frequent symptoms are a distraction, the flight of ideas, the alteration of judgment, anger, and aggressiveness, and the ideas of greatness. In the depressive phase, the mood is markedly depressed by sadness and unhappiness, with some degree of anxiety. Activity is usually decreased, but there may be restlessness and agitation. Also, there is a marked propensity for recurrence that, in some cases, can occur at regular intervals. As far as the regression of libido is concerned, it is a pathology linked to the oral-sadistic stage — second time of the oral phase, according to a subdivision introduced by K. Abraham in 1924, which coincides with the appearance of the teeth and bite activity — of the evolution of libido.

Schizophrenic psychosis - Term created by E. Bleuler (1911) to designate a group of psychoses, whose affinity had already been indicated by Kraepelin grouping them under the heading "early dementia", which in psychiatry, over time, have become classic: hebephrenic schizophrenia - the subject gradually loses the ability to plan and foresee the future, leading a wandering life without any purpose (they consider themselves great inventors and/or benefactors of humanity) ; catatonic schizophrenia - the subject falls into an alarming state of stupor without responding to the environment, a state that is intertwined with outbreaks of senseless excitement and hyperactivity; and paranoid schizophrenia - the subject develops a true delusional system in which everything revolves around himself: first, he feels observed, watched and controlled by one or more people; later, he becomes convinced that they persecute and harass him to kill him or make him suffer; Lastly, he folds back on himself and isolates himself from objective reality to live in a world of fantastic representations.

In general, we can say that schizophrenia is a mental illness characterized by the loss of the sense of reality, the predominance of the inner life and the presence of hallucinations, a disease that refers us to the oral phase of the evolution of libido — a phase in which sexual pleasure is linked to the excitation of the oral cavity and lips.

CHAPTER 9

CHALLENGE AND IMPROVE YOUR MIND

The most powerful faculty in our mind is its ability to stay focused. Improving our mental focus will allow us to benefit more.

Maintaining a higher mental focus minimizes the power of distractions and improves our performance. The good news is that each of us, with a little practice and insight, can improve our ability to focus.

With the mind, a maxim resembling that which works with our muscles may apply. The more you work on its abilities, the more strength you will gain. Improving mental focus is perfectly possible. But that does not mean that it is a simple and fast process. To achieve this, you will have to make conscious efforts to eliminate, change, or introduce new habits.

Assess your mental focus

Assessing your present condition is the first step to strengthening your mental concentration. It would help if you asked yourself some questions about that. Does your imagination stretch out to other horizons while doing an essential task? Do you ever get off track of what you've been doing? Need to start all over again? Will you have problems getting away from distractions? If you answer those questions in the affirmative, your mental concentration will need to be dramatically increased.

You also need to ask yourself about the level of

concentration you achieve when you perform tasks that test your abilities. Do you like setting goals and dividing tasks into more manageable segments? If you catch your mind wandering, will you take a break and go back to what you've been doing? During the time zones where you are most involved, do you appear to overcome the most difficult challenges?

Keep distractions away

Even if it seems obvious, eliminating distractions is fundamental to improving mental focus. The problem is that very often, we are not aware of the immense amount of distractions around us.

To do this, start by locating and minimizing sources of distraction. It sounds simple, but it isn't. Studies tell us that over the long term, this habit will become very profitable.

One thing to notice here is that the disturbances are not permanent at all. From outside, sounds and interruptions are always harder to handle than the things that circle in our ears. Especially disturbing and persistent can be exhaustion, worry, anxiety, lack of motivation, and other internal disorders.

To minimize internal distractions, it is important to make a list of everything we need to "let go" so as not to drag this fatigue behind us. Building on positive thoughts and affirmations is also a good strategy, especially when dealing with anxiety and concern.

Focus on one thing at a time

Multitasking is not effective, even if it might seem fantastic for our mental focus. It reduces productivity, and targeting the details to separate the most important from the superfluous becomes much more difficult because our attention has a limited capacity.

Part of enhancing your mental concentration is to take full advantage of the opportunities you have. So, you have to give up multitasking and pay attention to one thing (or one problem) in full.

Take breaks

After a while, your mental focus may start to "fill up with vices," becoming less and less effective. Ultimately, your performance is affected.

Traditional explanations of psychology have suggested that this is due to the depletion of attention resources. However, some researchers believe that this point is more related to the brain's tendency to change sources of stimulation.

It was discovered that with very brief pauses and by diverting attention to another point, the mental focus could improve. Thus, introducing "breathing moments " during activities that require a lot of concentration will help you considerably. In our agenda, it is essential to see moments of work and moments of diversion.

Train to strengthen your mental focus

There are two things to keep in mind: mental focus takes time; we will always have room to improve it. One of the first steps is to recognize the impact of distraction as a source of exhaustion. By changing your mental focus and following the strategies we have listed, you will discover that you can maintain a high level of attention. And this for longer.

Other things affect our mental focus. We think for example of our food or the quality of our sleep. By taking care of the influencing factors, direct and indirect, we will see how agile our mind can be.

CHAPTER 10

Why do people say YES

They don't want to do it and still do it. People who say yes when they mean no have a particular fear.

People who keep saying yes when they mean no want to keep the peace at all costs in the world and not be noticed negatively.

You prefer not to attract attention. Because if you stand out — in whatever form — it can always provoke conflicts of all kinds. So, it is not that some find the behavior useful, and others do not. That's why they just say "yes" as often as possible.

Notorious yes-man

"Can you still quickly ..." "Would you please ..." or "I still need you today for ..." The question is, it is simply an invitation for notorious yes-sayers to say yes? They adapt to any situation that may appear spontaneously and thus always serve others well. One could almost forget that these people still have their own lives — they always work perfectly and are available without any complaints.

However, their own needs are the very last place. And with that, unfortunately, that of their favorite people too. Does someone have to stay back and work overtime again? You don't have to think long about who to ask. Does anyone have to change their vacation schedule because of an urgent order? The name is programmed.

But why are they doing this? Because they're afraid of others' reactions. And this is immediately followed by the fear of rejection, which — like so many things — already arises in childhood.

A behavioral pattern in which you always say yes to others is, unfortunately, often the first step in burnout.

Relationships are chronically stressed

Anyone who thinks they have to say yes always and everywhere has another problem in addition to the organizational stress: They live in constant tension. Because it is never predictable when, where, and what they will be used for, and they will have to say yes again. And because it means that they always have difficulties in explaining to their loved ones.

So, if you take a close look at relationships, there is something very unhealthy about them. Because if you don't allow yourself to speak about your own needs in one relationship, but always orientate yourself towards the other, this relationship is very difficult.

Who feels addressed now: Set clear boundaries to the people who make demands on you that they cannot or do not want to meet now.

A healthy relationship is not characterized by constantly saying yes, but by the fact that a dialogue is possible.

So, if you are asked again whether you can stay longer today or do this or that service, you can say that it won't work. It is the most natural thing in the world to refuse a request —

for whatever reason. You can, but don't have to explain why. Sometimes a conversation is easier if you substantiate statements with reasons; for example, "Unfortunately, today it is not possible, I have to pick up my children from kindergarten" or "I have agreed to eat with my husband/wife for 6:00 p.m." etc. The "why" is none of their business, so you shouldn't justify reasons. It is also essential that you only say such reasons once and not always repeat them. The other one has already heard it.

Prepare for resistance

And to come back to the fear of the reaction of others — and thus the fear of rejection – mentioned above: Yes, the reaction of others will probably not be very pleasant because it has always worked wonderfully so far – you have always worked wonderfully, for others. If you are aware of this in advance, you can better deal with it if your counterpart may rebel and want to blame you or even feel guilty. You know that can happen, and therefore you can develop resistance to it.

Over time, however, you will notice that the more certain and confident you appear, the more other people will also accept and respect your rejections. And the quality of your relationships will improve because you meet other people at eye level.

Important: See every little "no" — however you put it – as your success, which will motivate you to say "yes" again next time – namely yes to yourself and your own needs.

Anyone who always wants to please everyone ensures that

everyone is fine but they themselves are miserable. Start today by standing by your own needs and standing up for them. If you are aware that a "no" can offend others and may surprise or even annoy them, you will know what is coming, and you can better deal with it.

Why we should say less, "yes, but."

Does this situation seem familiar to you? You are in the middle of intensive communication. Because you have a lot of ideas on the subject, you respond promptly with "Yes, but we also have to consider ..." "Yes, but shouldn't we ..." or " Yes, but that also includes ... "?

We all do this from time to time. And like to place this "yes but" between the execution of our interlocutor without letting him or her say it. We may then be surprised if our counterpart gets louder, discusses more heatedly and somehow seems very dissatisfied. There was no result, the ideas were really good, and the interest from both sides was honest.

What could have happened? Here's an idea: Even if you did not want it, you have signaled to your counterpart that you do not agree. A "yes but" may seem like an affirmative addition to an argument; every "yes but" is a sign to your conversation partners that they are wrong and have not considered certain things. Instead of "Yes" = confirmation and "but" = supplement, your counterpart hears "Yes" = "I heard you," "but" = "You are wrong." The "yes" opens the door so that you can kick your shin even better with the "but." Doesn't sound good, does it? By doing so, you force your counterpart into justification pressure. Instead of a solution-oriented discussion, an exchange of blows perceived as unpleasant develops.

Yes, I know you don't mean that. But it matters. "Yes, but"...

- ... are like a wall against which ideas bounce off.
- ... immediately redirect the dialog: "Stop, you can't get any further here."
- ... interrupt the flow of thought, and you always start over.
- ... do not continue an idea but oppose it.

It is like cooking - "Yes, but" pours the recipe into the sink because it has not yet been completed. On the other hand, if you added spice or another ingredient, you could enjoy a delicious meal. Such a perfection creates a "yes exactly" or "yes and" in conversation.

"Yes, exactly," or "Yes and" enrich the communication

These two formulations are invitations to think ahead. An almost revolutionary approach to positively receiving and spinning every impulse that is indispensable. If we replace "but" with "and," we achieve something big with a small change. The "and" connects, it places two viewpoints side by side, so that they can exist in parallel. The "but" is very different — it evaluates and contrasts your point of view with the other or even above the other.

We can achieve with a "yes and": We listen to each other and constructively pursue a common goal. New ideas will continue. You get the space that you deserve. A situation can relax; creativity grows. Beautiful right? Give it a try:

Discuss a topic with colleagues or friends, to solve a problem. For example, think about what you could do tonight. While you start each paragraph with "Yes but" in the first round, in the second round, you start your writings with "Yes and" or "Yes exactly." How does that feel?

Typically, the "yes exactly" round is much faster. The resulting common idea is much richer than the occasional split of ideas from the first round.

The decisive difference between "yes but" and "yes and": While "yes but" starts a new train of thought, "yes and" or "yes exactly" will always continue or supplement a train of thought. That is why in the end, a whole is created – regardless of whether it was a professional conversation or just the question of what you cook in the evening.

Let's take a look at this question in practice:

B: What are we eating tonight?

A: Do we want to make pizza?

B: Yes, but we already had it yesterday.

A: What do we want to do then, suggest something.

B: I don't know, suggest something.

A: ...

Scene change - same question again:

B: What are we eating tonight?

A: Do we want to make pizza?

B: Yes, exactly, and today we make them with tomatoes and

mozzarella, not like yesterday with ham and Edam, then it is lighter and tastes completely different.

Do you notice what happens? "Yes and" answers get to the goal faster, but they need a little more brainpower for the respondent. Perhaps it is because so often a "yes but" is used. There are other reasons for this.

Why we say "yes but" so often

- We have been brought up to be problem thinkers.

It is almost a good thing first to analyze, think through, organize and structure everything. If we have identified all potential gaps and eliminated all sources of error, we could come to a solution. For us, things are broken. First, glasses are usually half empty. The deficiency is omnipresent, and it needs to be remedied. In other words, we see problems as opportunities.

- We are security and preservation oriented

If you say "yes but," you can stay in your comfort zone, you have to move (mentally) less. It is not about problem-solving, but (unconsciously) about keeping the current state. The "yes but" practically blocks further development that creates security. It is good for everyone who is anxious and likes to have the situation under control. (And there are many, I would like to include myself in it!) Whoever does not want to dare is against it on principle and will feel more comfortable in "Yes but" than in "Yes and."

- We are trained to place our own opinion in the best possible way.

With the "yes," yes-sayers initially agree to speak. And because they are better informed, they always have an objection, have legitimate doubts and can argue against something. In doing so, they manifest their expert status as "know-it-all," drawing everyone's attention. They are the focus and enjoy their special position, however, at the expense of the result.

What do we say about ourselves when we say "yes but"?

Language is more than the transmission of information. You have heard of the factual level and the relationship level. If you have followed the explanations so far, you will have realized that a "yes but" transports little on the factual level and a lot on the relationship level. If you want to eradicate it, with yourself and with others, you can work on the relationship. And also on yourself. I dare to guess: Those who are at peace with themselves say less "yes but" and more often dare to say "yes and" to a situation or the other person.

CHAPTER 11

HOW TO GAIN AN ADVANTAGE OVER ANYONE'S MIND

You wanted to know what someone was doing hundreds of times. To know what a person thinks is an advantage for a better understanding, attracting, selling, revealing criminals, and many other benefits, both positive and not so positive.

To know how to benefit from people's, men's, or women's minds is not something magical, but one must be careful about the conclusions reached. In general, the more observant and interested you are, the more effective you are in reading others' thoughts.

On the other hand, one does not know exactly what someone feels that takes advantage of the mind. You won't hear a sound in your mind if you don't have a sixth sense — telepathy.

The aim is to analyze people's behavior and deduce their feelings, state of mind, and thinking. Also, the meaning would be essential as well. Many solutions will be more probable than others, depending on the situation.

Although you know it, you already take advantage of the mind

We would not be able to handle social situations or develop personal relationships with others without knowing other people's feelings or ideas.

The theory of mind is an ability that arises from 3 to 4 years of age and relates to other people's ability to relate thoughts and intentions.

If a person has developed this capability, he can understand and think about his personal and other mental conditions.

According to the University of Texas researcher, William Ickes, foreigners can "scan" each other with 20% accuracy and friends and partners with 35% accuracy. Those who have built this capacity are as high as 60%.

How to learn to take advantage of the mind:

-Begin by knowing yourself

How do you know what other people are if you don't know yourself? It is not a single, but a dynamic process that we know what others think or feel.

To begin with, you should know how you are feeling at any moment — your inner state.

The more you are conscious of yourself, the more you recognize your mental state. And you or your interlocutor can contribute to this state of mind.

Negative emotions are more communicated than positive, so that's a way to know how you feel with whom you speak.

Have you spoken to a person with "good vibes" transmitted to you? And did you speak to someone who expressed stresses or negative emotions to you?

It's mentally tainted. The more you know your mental condition, the happier you are.

Anything that can assist you is mindfulness or meditation, strategies that let you learn about the "inner world."

Remember that you won't realize what the other person thinks without interacting.

You would, therefore, need to communicate with yourself. There are more positive ways in this case than others:

Good: it seems that you feel a bit sad. Am I wrong? Am I right?

Bad: I know what you think / you sound like me.

-Read lips

This part is due to the experience of FBI agent Jack Shafer.

Pucker your lips slightly

A gesture that shows you disagree a little with the clearing of your lips. The more it is, the more the discord.

Pursed lips indicate that the person produced a thought that was contradictory to what was said or done.

If, for example, you want to convince someone, it's a trick to "change your mind" before you can convey your opposition verbally.

Once a person expresses their opinions publicly, the psychological concept known as consistency makes it very difficult to change his views.

It causes much less psychological stress to retain a position than to make continuous decisions, regardless of the arguments.

Lip biting

A common way of "reading the mind" is to see as the speaker mugs his mouth. It consists of the lower or the upper lip with a soft bite.

This gesture means, though he doesn't dare, that someone wants to say something; usually, people don't say what they think because they believe they offend others.

You can communicate more effectively if you know what your partner or friends do not dare to say. One way is to state with empathy what you believe causes fear.

For example:

You: Do you agree that we should spend more time together

He/she: No, I want you to help me in my house.

Press the lips

This happens if you combine the upper and lower lip, pinch the mouth, and darken the lips. This compression is a sense of biting the lips, although it has a more negative significance.

This happens anytime someone needs to say something but twists their lips not to say it. In clear empathic comments, you can persuade a suspect to bear witness:

"You've got to say something, but you don't want to think about it."

Here are some tricks:

If you see pickled lips, "change the person's mind" before

he expresses his objections.

Use a compassionate statement to learn why the person is anxious about what you are saying when you see bitten and pressed lips.

-Work empathy

You don't have a link to other people's emotions if you use your brain to think about the future, the past, or your problems.

It is how the subconscious senses the thoughts of other people. And even if you're not looking after it, you have the potential.

Today students at college exhibit 40 percent less empathy than those from the 1980s and 1990s, according to Sara Konrath of the University of Michigan.

However, while empathy can be overlooked, everyone can grow it and apply it.

Your brain is empathetic; when someone you are watching is acting, you have neurons called "mirror nerves."

These neurons play an important role in linking the emotions and thoughts of other people besides socializing.

Have you happened to walk down the road, meet someone, and decide to go in the same direction and block you were coming from?

This is because your mirror neurons imitate the other person's behavior until the information is processed, and the opposite movement is carried out by your mind.

Christian Keysers from the University of Groningen says that you feel fear or disgust when you see a spider creeping up your leg.

Likewise, you feel your emotions as if you're there when you watch your soccer and basketball team lose or win.

When you watch others, you will experience social emotions such as shame, anger, pride, or lust.

To increase your empathy follow these steps:

Live now: The more your brain is, the more you can sense your thoughts and those of the other person, the more you worry about the past or future. Therapy is a good practice. Practice watching people and the environment without considering anything else.

You can watch movies that tell plays or humorous people's stories. Watch and listen. The links in the emotional brain are enhanced by being interested in someone else's life. It's still better in a theatre. However, the best way to meet friends or relatives is to listen to one another face to face and pay full attention without interruption.

Ask yourself what you feel: Your self-awareness will strengthen your understanding of other people. You will ask yourself what you expect. Stand three to four times a day, wondering: How do I feel? Right now, what's my emotion? Also, find out where you feel your emotions in the body. For starters, where do you feel anxiety or fear? In the chest? Arms?   The neck?

Check the intuition. Tell them the feeling that you feel or try to find out what you feel if you talk to someone. If you see, for example, your boyfriend looks animated, say to him: 'Is something good happening to you? You look very animated.'

-Eye contact

Vision is a human being's most essential feeling.

According to a study by the University of Miami, the importance of the eyes in communicating with others is so important that 43.4% of our attention towards someone else is focused on their eyes.

You can deduce what a person feels or schemes from a person's eyes. You will find out more about this topic in this chapter.

To blink

The frequency of blinking can alter emotions toward another human.

It can indicate that you are drawn to your speaker when you blink more than 6-10 times per minute.

Blinking more can also show the person's nervousness.

Since 1980, the person who blinked the most lost in presidential debates.

Raise eyebrows

People lift their eyes when they want a better understanding of themselves.

It also shows compassion, empathy, and a willingness to get

along.

Squint

Squinting means distrust or unbelief and is an often-involuntary expression.

Gaze direction

After the NLP was first identified, several people have written about the direction that the eyes look to.

The contact model helps you recall everything looking to the left.

In comparison, looking to the right means that thoughts or images are produced, which some people interpret as lying.

Note: it's the other way around for lefties.

Pupils

In 1975 Eckhard Hess found that when an individual is interested in others, the pupils dilate.

The pupils contract when we see situations that disgust us. Dilation: the pupil's size increases. Contraction: the pupil is reduced in size.

-Mind activity is more difficult; the pupils dilate more. Nevertheless, pupils are limited when mental activity is too high.

-As we experience pain, they dilate.

Seduction

There appears to be a consensus in flirtation and seduction that:

-When the other party does not respond to you and initiates contact, they might not be involved.

You leave him/her uncomfortable if you continue to look at him/her after he or she turns away or fails to look around.

-The other person is probably going to feel comfortable and react positively if you start eye contact.

Boys may take account of the following:

1) When a girl looks you in the eye, looking away and then going back to your eyes; surely she's interested.

2) When she breaks eye contact and looks out, nothing is certain.

3) If you take care to make eye contact, you're probably not interesting.

For girls who want to seduce with their eyes: For a man to start knowing that she is interested, he requires an average of three glances from a girl.

Dominance

Rich, high-ranking individuals or others who choose to show dominance tend to have less eye contact.

To look elsewhere is another way of showing dominance.

Avoid eye contact

Avoiding looking into other people's eyes may indicate that they are ashamed for some reason.

Therefore, avoiding interaction with anyone else also means being frustrated.

You must also bear in mind that the contact time is culturally important. In New York, for example, 1.68 seconds is acceptable.

The 'Reading The Mind in the Eyes Test,' is a psychologic test created by the University of Cambridge's Simon Baron-Cohen that enhances your ability to read thoughts.

-Other keys of non-verbal language

Are you aware that non-verbal language dictates 93 percent of the strength of human communication?

The influence and impact of our communication are determined by:

- Non-verbal: 55%
- Paralinguistic elements: 38%
- Oral content: 7%

There are certain aspects that you should consider in this subject:

Touch the nose and cover the mouth: People tend to cover the mouth and touch the nose when they are lying. The adrenaline in the capillaries of the nose could be increased. On the other hand, it would be the aim to bring the hands close to the mouth.

Unrest: When a person searches out something or his body is still moving around. It is presumed that anxieties that are released from physical movements that affect part of the body compulsively are generated by telling a lie. The issue is whether the behavior, as a person normally does, is different.

Speak slowly: The person can pause to find something to say by telling a lie.

Throat: A lying person can constantly swallow.

The expression is confined to the mouth: When someone forges emotions (happiness, shock, sorrow ...), the face only shifts at the mouth: the chin, the eyes, and the front.

Microexpressions are facial expressions that are almost invisible and shown by people as they occur in a split second. Some can detect them, but most of them can't. The microexpression of an individual lies in a stress emotion characterized by raised eyebrows that create expression lines on the front.

Knowing all the signs of non-verbal language is very extensive.

CHAPTER 12

HOW QUICKY CAN I LEARN NLP?

While respecting the person as he is (both cognitive, emotional, and behavioral), NLP gives us the keys to "being at best with yourself," associating things that happen with positive, taking a step back to avoid feeling the negative emotional impact.

This can help in many situations where one may encounter difficulties: to be comfortable during a presentation of an important issue at work, be quiet and available for the children's homework, be full of energy in the morning upon waking, or remain attentive and kind to a client or an angry person.

- Exercise 1: anchoring

The objective of this Exercise

Anchoring is a natural process that unconsciously and automatically associates an internal reaction with an external stimulus: a hello, a wink, a "top there" during an agreement reached. We memorize these links and thus create what are called "anchors." As soon as an anchor is stimulated, the feeling experienced in the past returns instantly.

The anchors can be visual (a seashell in your bathroom reminds you of holidays in Mauritius), auditory (this piece of music, a romantic moment), kinesthetic (this ball in the stomach, this moment of panic during of an examination), olfactory (this delicious smell of chocolate, your childhood in your grandmother's house) or gustatory (the most famous description of a gustatory anchor is, of course, Proust's madeleine!).

Instructions for use

Think of a situation where you feel an unpleasant internal state and ask yourself which positive internal state (a memory, a place that calms you ...) do you want to be in this situation?

Stressed out — you want to be relaxed, anxious — you want to be serene or full of self-confidence.

Once you have chosen your desired internal state, follow this procedure:

- **Sit in a quiet place, close your eyes, and find a memory where you experienced this positive internal state**. Relive the scene by being fully associated with it, until you feel it completely in your body.

- **Anchor the positive internal state**. In this situation, the kinesthetic anchor is the most effective. For example, you can clench your fist or stimulate a point on the body (wrist, knee, ear, etc.) for at least 20 seconds. Repeat this operation 2 to 3 times to reinforce the anchor in place.

- **Test the impact of the anchor.** Forget the previous steps for a moment and think of something else. Then once in a neutral internal state, stimulate the anchor in place and let the positive internal state return.

- **While stimulating the anchor, project yourself into the**

future in a difficult context. And let yourself experience what this positive internal state now allows you to do and your new behaviors ...

This magic button is now at your disposal to help you in difficult situations. But an anchor wears out if you don't use it! Remember to activate it regularly and strengthen it by stimulating it in new situations where you experience this positive internal state.

- Exercise 2: Submodalities

The objective of this Exercise

The "submodalities" represent how the brain sorts and codifies experience. By modifying the structure of our experience, it is possible to modify the experience itself and our emotional and behavioral reactions.

The sensory representations are all different: a mental image can be pale or dark, large or small, in color or black and white. In the same way, an auditory representation has a certain volume or rhythm.

How to use

Now learn to juggle submodalities. Take an unpleasant task and a pleasant task. For example, you hate ironing or filing your tax return but love to garden. Make a representation of these two experiences. Now go through your submodality checklist and fill in your table.

Look at your two columns and identify the differences. This is called doing contrast analysis.

You will now transform your unpleasant task and make it pleasant by playing with your submodalities: give your negative representation the pleasant task's components!

Among your parameters, there are undoubtedly 1 or 2, which will have a dominant impact: it is the critical submodality (often it is a question of size or distance). Now look at this "redesigned" representation: your motivation and your feelings are likely very different.

- Exercise 3: Swish

The objective of this Exercise

The word swish means "whistling" or "rustling," like the noise of an image which would quickly cover another.

This technique makes it possible to modify a person's internal representations and transform a negative feeling into a positive feeling. This is to short-circuit the trigger of the anxiety-provoking situation.

It is appropriate whenever an internal image triggers an unpleasant feeling: stage fright, malaise, anxiety, lack of confidence, demotivation ... It can also be used in addictive behaviors.

Instructions

- Identify the problematic situation: In which situation do you want to react differently?

- Identify the image linked to the problem: Locate the internal image that you see in this situation just before having the attitude you want to change. Identify the internal manifestations that this negative image triggers in you.

- Create a positive image: Let a second image come, an image of you having full self-confidence. To serve in all circumstances, this image must be dissociated (you can see yourself as if we had taken a photo of you) and not contextualized. Modify this image so that it is really attractive and gives you positive bodily reactions, a feeling of well-being, and fulfillment.

- The swish: Close your eyes and view the first image. It must be large and clear. Then place a small dark image at the bottom left, your 2nd positive image. Grow this little image that lights up as it covers the other, while the first image shrinks and becomes dark. Start again by repositioning your two images and do these 5 or 6 times in succession faster and faster. At the end of this process, visualize a white screen and open your eyes.

- Test the result: Turn the screen back on and look at the image before you. Can you find the first image? What difference does it make?

- Project into the future: Imagine yourself in a few weeks in a situation similar to the one you mentioned at the start... How does this new person you have become behaves? What do you feel? What can you now do in different contexts of your life?

Manipulate the mind through Dark NLP

NLP's bad reputation is well known. It can be used to manipulate people and influence them against their will.

Others think that it is valuable to help and has made them happier both professionally and personally. So what is really behind these three letters?

Neuro-linguistic programming – the explanation of the abbreviation. Translated, it means "the new formation of the connections between nerves and language." There is a complex idea behind it. It is about recognizing old patterns of thought, both for myself and my counterpart, to break them down and transform them into new ones that are more suitable for me or others.

NLP was developed by the then math student and later psychologist Richard Bandler and the linguist John Grinder in the early 1970s at the University of California in Santa Cruz. They wanted to use it to design new short-term psychotherapy.

The method is based on observing people who are particularly successful in different areas and filtering out commonalities. These successful behaviors can be learned separately from others.

To achieve this, there are various basic assumptions and techniques in the NLP:

Although basic assumptions cannot be directly proven, they serve as the basis for a thought model. Every community has such so-called postulates. In the NLP, this would be, for example, "Behind every behavior, there is a positive intention." What may seem surprising at first glance makes sense on closer inspection. Imagine a teenage boy stealing from someone. If you ask for the reason, he will first say that he wanted this item. Upon closer inquiry, however, it soon becomes clear that he wanted to impress his friends and thus belong to the group. These basic needs for recognition, security, and belonging are our strongest drives. This idea is not to excuse any action, but it should enable positive behavior that meets the same basic needs.

Further postulates would then be:

- "Every behavior is useful in a certain context."
- "There is no failure, only feedback."
- "People always make the best decision available to them."

To expand this available choice of decision options, NLP now has different techniques, but they all have the same basic structure.

Pacing - Outing - Leading

To be able to communicate successfully with a person, rapport must be established. If we want to communicate with someone, we create a subconscious rapport. If you want to design this process consciously, you have to consider the following stages:

Pacing, also called mirroring, is the first stage. You try to adapt yourself as well as possible to your counterpart, i.e., imitate posture, language style, etc. This happens automatically when we meet up with good friends.

Outing describes the conscious perception of one's sensations that have arisen through pacing. This is also a good tool for a quick check of your counterpart's situation in everyday life. Try it! Sit up straight, shoulders back, head raised – how do you feel? So, you can see that our posture already says a lot about how we are doing.

Leading - Once we have established a good connection with our counterpart, we can try to help them, because only if we have won their trust will they be ready to accept our help.

The subsequent change work can now be done in different ways. It is impossible to give a complete treatise since NLP has always been based on a wide variety of therapy concepts. The Gestalt therapist Fritz Perls was particularly influenced by the family therapist Virginia Satir and the hypnotherapist Milton H. Erickson.

The problem with NLP is that there is no clear theoretical framework. We therefore often find a mixture, especially with various esoteric teachings.

NLP was not designed to manipulate people. The goal was to help them faster and more efficiently than ever before. It opens up countless new opportunities and is a great tool. But just because a tool could be dangerous, we don't throw all knives out of the kitchen. And just because a doctor could kill us, we don't refuse to go back to the doctor when we are in pain.

As with any tool, it depends on which hands it comes in, and we should never stop thinking critically about the things we encounter. It can then advance each individual in their personal development and help us significantly improve communication with our fellow human beings!

CHAPTER 13

THE TRUE STORY OF BRAINWASHING & HOW IT SHAPED THE WORLD

One of the "classics" in the History of "Brainwashing" is to believe that it does not exist. Architects of this "classic" officiate as preachers willing to proclaim to the four winds that no one is brainwashed.

One of the main detergents of this "washing" system is the fear that, whether with biblical genesis or with nuclear warheads, it presses our lives, minute by minute, to make us happy and obedient to everything that exploits us, humiliates and neutralizes us. It is about erasing all critical, organizing, and mobilizing thinking and methods ready to transform the monstrous reality perpetrated by capitalism. They show it on TV.

Today, all intimidation operations (always invented) seem like child's play alongside the images perpetrated by Gaza's bombings, the ISIS paraphernalia, and the macabre deployment amplified by the alliance between "organized crime" and the bourgeois mass media. The seven deadly sins and Orson Wells seem like fairy tales. At the end of the discourse, reigns — unpunished — the moral that shows the power of harm to subject us to deception. Isn't that why the crucified Christ is exposed to the dead?

The "acute" phase is when the victim becomes wilful and takes the initiative to wash her brain alone and wash it promptly to her "loved ones." She learns to brainwash meticulously, with determination and good humour, making it a moralizing exhibition among her own and others. The collaborative and sustainable attitude that saves the bourgeoisie many expenses. The acute phase is expressed at ease when the victims are grateful (intimately and in the public square) for being victimized and recognize that the victimizer was always right and continues to be right. Mission accomplished.

Brainwashing has taken modern forms and has been institutionalized according to the specialties demanded by the imperialism market. The laundries of brains concentrated in the plunder of natural resources and particularly plunder of oil. "It is for your good," they say, "it is because you do not know how to take advantage of it," "you do not have the technology or understand it," "it is progress," "it is modern," "it is transparent" ... "it is inevitable." There are jewels of cynicism and self-confidence enshrined in contracts, agreements, alliances, and decrees with many clappers with or without wages.

At the top of the brainwashes are the recently visible "vulture funds" that have made the verb "pay" a dogma with unprecedented fanaticism chained to ancient traditions. No matter the caliber of the aberrations it implies, you have to pay because the "judges" say so. Not only the "judges" subservient to capitalism but the hierarchical "judges" of bourgeois morality who regulate the quality of honesty with the amount of what is paid and brainwash us to "honor the debt." It does not matter if we walk into the abyss of the worst crisis of misery and dispossession that we could have imagined... they want us to pay with a brainwashed mind ready to meet the next payments set for eternity.

We will not say that they did not warn us. We have centuries of inventions and havoc in the art of brainwashing. There are schools, debates, and diverse tendencies that, to which more, dispute the paternity of one or another "technique" better to stop an efficient and thorough washing. There are specialized universities, and there are awards with planetary prestige for those who, in whole or part, perfect brainwashing in their individual or mass versions. Churches and sects have, in this notable circle, their "number seats" even though it is increasingly difficult to distinguish them from bourgeois television channels, some political parties, and some scientific research and teaching centers.

The Battle of Ideas is the class struggle expressed in thought for revolutionary action. Our anti-capitalist and world struggle must understand that the transformation of the world lies in modifying the relations of production and the ideas about the reality for the egalitarian and just life in collective. Thus, it is necessary to identify and deactivate all the weapons of ideological warfare that the bourgeoisie has invented and prepare ourselves to develop antidotes as strategies with revolutionary methods of simultaneous thought and action.

Living as mourners will be useless to us, no matter how effective our analyzes and claims are. It is time to move forward and not stay in the complaint, in the observation, or the diagnosis because it is urgent to integrate all our best strengths into a creative unity and struggle program that gives the production of ideas its forced and indissoluble place in the production of actions.

CHAPTER 14

IS HYPNOSIS REAL?

We have all heard of hypnosis. But the image that has usually been given to this technique is something mystical that drives you to do strange things, or something typical of quacks who want to deceive us. What is hypnosis? Does it work? Why is it not effective for everyone? Here we reveal it to you.

It is not true that you are at the mercy of the hypnotist, and that, for example, you are capable of killing a person in a trance. First of all, your rational capacity continues to function, although in a different way.

Not all people can be hypnotized equally. And this is because they have different brain structures. Also, hypnosis has effects at the brain level, causing changes in its functioning.

Hypnosis can be defined as a state of consciousness during which a person has intensified attention and concentration, allowing him to explore his thoughts, talents, and experiences that are not normally accessible to us. Many professionals in psychology and psychiatry consider it a useful, scientifically supported technique with the ability to treat medical and psychological conditions.

Why can't all people be hypnotized?

Not all people are susceptible to being hypnotized since some are more suggestible than others. Therefore, it is essential to know if a person can be hypnotized before starting hypnotherapy since this technique may not work.

According to a study, people who cannot be put into a hypnotic trance have less connectivity in the areas associated with executive control (planning, organization, short-term memory) and attention than highly hypnotizable people. These people may be less able to allow themselves to be absorbed by day-to-day experiences, in which attention, action planning is coupled.

However, it has recently been seen that it is possible to improve people's hypnotic capacity by stimulating certain areas of the brain.

What happens in the brain during hypnosis?

Less activity in the brain area related to rationality:

According to a study, during the hypnotic process, activity in the brain area related to rational cognitive functions decreases. During hypnosis, we make less use of rationality, planning, we get carried away, and we stop worrying.

Greater mind-body connection

Also, in this study, an increase in the connections between two brain areas (dorsolateral cortex and the insula) was observed, which allows the brain to process and control what is happening in the body. Hypnosis gives us more control over our bodies.

Fewer connections between actions and action consciousness:

Another finding was the decrease in the connections between two areas involved in action consciousness and the action itself. When we are committed and involved with something, we don't think about doing it or how, we just carry it out. That is, during hypnosis, we are less aware of our actions. We are allowed to be more involved in the activities that are suggested to us or that we suggest to ourselves, saving us the mental resources that are put in place when we are fully aware of the activity.

However, it is not that you lose control; on the contrary, people feel much more control over their sensory, motor, and body functions. What happens is that they do it in an involuntary sense, as if they were simply observed doing it but without participating.

Facilitates deep sleep

According to a study, listening to audios before bedtime hypnotics significantly increases the amount of produced slow waves during deep sleep. This indicates that hypnosis also provides great levels of relaxation, improving the quality of sleep.

What can hypnosis be used for?

In easily hypnotizable patients, this technique effectively relieves chronic pain, labour pain, treating tobacco addiction, post-traumatic stress disorder, and improving symptoms of anxiety, phobias, and sleep disorders. It has also been seen as effective in treating dementia symptoms.

History of Hypnosis

The first manifestations of hypnosis already occurred, in the form of self-hypnosis, among the primitive men, who, with their mysterious songs, their ritual dances, enigmatic passes, and words, made spells regarding magical powers. Thus, they became collectively desensitized to pain, had visions and overcame tiredness, cured functional disorders, and reached cataleptic states. This was the beginning of magic, the appearance of healers and healing sorcerers who exerted great influence on the tribe.

There is evidence that hypnosis was already used in ancient Egypt, specifically in Ebers. In a papyrus of more than 3,000 years old, studied by Bordeaux, it is indicated that hypnosis was used, with induction techniques very different from those we currently use, to lead subjects to deep states of drowsiness. In the bas-relief of a tomb of Thebes, we see an Egyptian priest hypnotizing a person. Hypnosis spread to everyone.

In Greece, these suggestion techniques were so effective that special temples called "sleep temples" began to be erected, in which Asclepios (Aesculapius), God of Medicine, was worshiped.

In India, it became completely dominated. Through the repetition of mantras and the techniques of suggestion, the yogis managed to dominate the state of self-hypnosis.

Mesmer (born in 1734 in Germany, Ph.D. in Philosophy and Medicine) very influenced by the theories of Paracelsus, who claimed that there was etheric energy creating matter (later called "magnetic force") that penetrated everything and exerted great influence on men began using magnets, was advised by the Jesuit Father Hell, to control the magnetic force and use its healing powers. After his first important cure in 1773 of a young woman named Francisca Oesterling, who suffered from fainting, urine retention, melancholy and temporary paralysis, among other symptoms, Mesmer soon filled her with magnets (she even had one on her neck) with which she achieved cures (surely due to suggestion).

During the treatment, Mesmer turns a vat (he built his famous bucket or health vat, a large wooden container, inside which he puts bottles with water magnetized by him. From the bottles come large rods that patients apply to the different parts of the body) observing the healing of the sick, from the infinitely poor to the richest. The more successful he was, the greater the Faculty of Medicine's complaints, which accused him of departing from traditional teachings.

In 1777, he cured Maria Teresa Paradis, daughter of the Ambassador of Vienna's secretary and goddaughter of the Empress, of blindness started at four years of age. Mesmer put her under treatment, providing a full recovery, but the blindness manifested again (suggesting hysterical blindness). A great scandal arose, joined by his medical rivals, and he had to leave for Paris.

In Paris, the success was not small, and Mesmer began to earn a lot of money. As planned, the doctors rejected his proposals. The first protests were not long in coming, which ended in a great scandal. Individuals, societies, and sects (including Freemasonry) unconditionally sided with him:

"War on the Academy."

Upon verifying Mesmer's great prestige and his "miraculous cures," Louis XIV asked the Academy of Sciences for an official magnetism report. A report that declared the absence of any magnetic fluid and that "magnetism without imagination produces absolutely nothing."

An outstanding disciple of Mesmer, Puységur, magnetized a tree (an elm), and the sick who came to him fell asleep quickly.

In 1813, a priest from Portuguese India appeared, Father Faria. Faria denied the magnetic fluid existence and demonstrated it in public exhibitions in which he stared at a subject and shouted "Fall asleep!" His fascination called this induction system. From Faria, things began to clear up, and scientific hypnosis appeared, and it is based on the fact that everything consists of a psychophysiological state. However, the above trajectory should not be underestimated as it reveals the power of suggestion.

In 1819, a Catalan dentist surnamed Martorell, and a resident in Paris, was the first to remove a tooth without pain.

Scottish surgeon James Braid (1795-1861), after some experiences with his wife and assistant, formulated the following theory: "The sustained fixation on a person's gaze paralyzes the nervous centers of the eyes, destroying the balance of the nervous system and producing the dream state." Braid gave the name of hypnotism to this state.

Liebault, a young doctor at the French Academy of Sciences,

after reading Braid's works, began working with hypnosis. His colleagues soon called him a charlatan, and even Bernheim went looking for him to humiliate him. But he was so surprised by what he saw that he joined him and together they formed Nancy's first school of hypnotism, where Bernheim published The Suggestion. These two doctors claimed that hypnosis is as effective as it is harmless.

Meanwhile, in Paris, Charcot experimented with Salpêtriere's hysterics, although he did not hypnotize but one of his students. Charcot sent a report to the Paris Academy of Medicine in 1882, in which he divided hypnosis into three states: lethargic, cataleptic, and sleepwalking. After being systematically rejected, hypnosis was finally recognized in the official scientific world. However, Charcot defined hypnosis as a symptom of hysteria. Hypnosis entered a moment of confusion.

In Spain, Ramón y Cajal proved to have a remarkable personal influence on his patients' imagination, and the success of hysteria and neurosis was so great that he had to close the office for lack of time to attend to people.

Already occupying the chair in Barcelona, his wife becomes pregnant with her sixth child. Silveria, who trusted him fully, allowed herself to be prepared and hypnotized when the time came, and in this way, her last two children were born.

Sigmund Freud at a conference in 1910 declared: "The history of psychoanalysis's genesis will never weigh the importance of hypnotism. In both the theoretical and

215

therapeutic sense, psychoanalysis administers an inheritance that hypnotism transmitted to it."

After attending a hypnotist session during his student years, he became interested in the therapeutic possibilities of hypnosis when Breuer informs him about his hypnotic experiences in Anna "O.."

His stay in Paris and his relationship with Charcot and Bernheim made him aware of these possibilities. From 1886 he became a strong advocate of hypnotism in the German-speaking medical world. By 1887 he began to use the hypnotic suggestion, initially with the Bernheim procedure and later with Breuer's so-called "cathartic technique."

Between 1892 and 1896, he developed the method of free association, taking advantage of hypnosis experiences and technical aspects, especially Berheim's demonstrations of the possibilities of recovering memories of the hypnotic state during the waking state through voluntary concentration.

At the age of twenty-nine Freud had spent six months at Charcot's office where he was impressed by the reality of the hypnotic phenomenon, later he continued to train Nancy where he wrote: "I witnessed extraordinary experiences regarding the possibilities opened up by the powerful psychic procedures that, they were hidden from the conscience of man."

Later, together with Breuer, he established the ideas of hypnotic regression and dynamic psychotherapy. Psychoanalytic theory suggests that hypnosis is a regression state in which the patient does not have the controls present in normal waking consciousness, and therefore acts impulsively and engages in fantasy production.

Freud abandons hypnotic ritual methods, surely because he was a bad hypnotist, very abrupt, simple, and authoritarian, but also because he was afraid of transference phenomena that he could not control.

From his hypnosis experience, the conviction that the patient has all the necessary elements for his healing, was important to get him to express himself freely to help him free his unconscious.

After Freud, the study and use of hypnosis go through a dark stage except for a few words. The appearance of psychoanalysis and pharmacological anesthesia contribute to this fact.

An honorable exception is the work of Clark Hull (1933), this neo-behaviorist author takes up Berheim's ideas and postulates the absence of qualitative differences between suggestion and hypnosis. In "Hypnosis and Suggestionability," he explains how there are only quantitative differences between suggestibility in the hypnotic state and the waking state. For him, we must speak of suggestion and hypnosis from a perspective based on Pavlov's inherited experimental psychology (who had explained hypnosis as a phenomenon of cortical inhibition), placing special emphasis on the subject's responses to certain demands of the ambient.

Numerous authors throughout the 20th century have

attached importance to the role of suggestion and suggestibility in psychology such as Binet (1900), Eysenck and Funrneaux (1945), Benton, and Bandura (1953), Stuark (1958), among others.

During World War II, the need for rapid and effective interventions revived interest in hypnosis. As a consequence, in the late 1940s, professional societies were founded with their respective publications: The Society for Clinical and Experimental Hypnosis (SCEH 1949) with the "The Journal of Clinical and Experimental Hypnosis," the International Society for Clinical and Experimental Hypnosis (ISH 1958) with the "International Journal of Clinical and Experimental Hypnosis," and the American Society of Clinical Hypnosis (ASCH, 1958) with the "American Journal of Clinical Hypnosis."

From the 1950s onwards, there was a revival, this time in the USA. Authors such as TX Barber, Martin Orne, William Kroger, Herbert Spiegel, ER Hilgard, TR Sarbin, Spanos, Chavez, Etzel Cardeña, Ph.D., among others, have been responsible for the increase in interest and the use of hypnosis, especially as a result of the influence of Dr. Milton H. Erickson and his work, which deserves a separate chapter in the historical evolution of Clinical Hypnosis.

Currently, the study and research in these areas are in a good moment. Over the past decades, prominent international groups of health professionals have publicly expressed their appreciation of hypnosis's therapeutic utility, including the American Medical Association, the British Medical Association, and the American Psychological

Association.

The creation of the American Society of Clinical Hypnosis under division 30 of the APA (created in 1973) and the European Society of Hypnosis in Psychotherapy and Psychosomatic Medicine reinforce and incorporate numerous professionals' therapeutic and experimental scientific activity. The definitive entry of hypnosis into experimental psychology laboratories begins the period of the so-called Scientific Hypnosis based on the work of, especially three laboratories that will defend their perspectives, that of Hilgard founded in 1957 at Stanford University, which studies the hypnosis relationships with variables such as age, sex, personality characteristics, etc. Barber's (1959) at the Medfield Foundation of the Massachusetts Hospital studied the role and effects of imagination, expectations, beliefs, motivations, and emotions on the ability to be hypnotized and the psychophysiological reactions produced by hypnotic suggestions. Finally, Orne's founded in 1960 at Harvard University, later transferred to the Hospital of the University of Pennsylvania, dedicated to studying the motivational factors of hypnosis and different hypnotic phenomena such as hypnotic regression production of amnesia and hypermnesia.

All three groups have developed scales to measure suggestibility (e.g., Weizenhoffer and Hilgard 1959, 1962; Shor and Orne 1962; Barber and Wilson, 1978).

This state of the situation has brought the consolidation of the so-called Experimental Hypnosis, which studies the phenomena of hypnosis in a laboratory situation and will frequently qualify and criticize the results obtained in the clinical or applied field so-called Clinical Hypnosis.

CONCLUSION

Are you afraid of having a conflict with your friend or another significant one? Do you make bad choices to please him? Will you tell little white lies to avoid problems? Can you blame him for his unhappiness? Rush to pamper him when he's getting irritated? Do you suffer and give, give, give, and feel sad and lonely, anyway?

You might be under an expert's thumb at emotional manipulation.

An emotional manipulator (EM) unconsciously and often subconsciously regulates and manipulates others' emotions for his gain. He wants to take control and have power over you. He employs understated methods, often without you knowing it, to change your perceptions. Qualified emotional manipulators will get you to give up your emotional self-esteem. Once you put your well being into an EM's hands, he will try to get control over you, methodically chipping away until there's very little left of the original.

How can that happen to you, and what kind of person becomes a manipulator of emotions? He makes use of underhanded methods.

Many EM's are narcissistic and feel a sense of entitlement because of their upbringing or genetics or a combination of both. As children, they may have been subjected to similar emotional abuse by their parents. Or, oddly enough, those kids could have been over-indulged or neglected. Extremes of either can in later life push a child into narcissism.

The entitlement of a narcissist makes them feel they should have what they wish without earning it. They don't need to take responsibility for themselves or their behavior. They don't have to be honest or treat other people fairly. It all has to do with them and what the world has done to them.

So how can a pretty person like you fall under an emotional manipulator 's spell?

You might be co-dependent and attracted to an emotional manipulator. You don't like to be alone either. If you are co-dependent, you'll need people to be helped. You feel the need to take care of anybody. And the emotional manipulator needs somebody to look after him.

It is so easy to fall for the EM who instantly develops trust with you. He shares with you deep emotions, and you perceive him to be delightfully sensitive, open, and perhaps a little vulnerable. You want to help him. And slowly you're getting engaged.

You are hooked after that, and you don't even notice that you are being manipulated emotionally.

www.ingramcontent.com/pod-product-compliance
Lightning Source LLC
Chambersburg PA
CBHW060317030426
42336CB00011B/1098